AMERICAN
HEROES

This edition published in 1988 by Gallery Books
An imprint of W.H. Smith Publishers Inc.
112 Madison Avenue
New York, New York, 10016

By arrangement with Octopus Books Ltd.

Copyright © 1988 Octopus Books Ltd.

Cover illustration by Hemesh A. Alles

ISBN 0 8317 0301 6

Printed in Czechoslovakia

AMERICAN
HEROES

Michael Johnstone

Illustrated by
Michael Strand

GALLERY BOOKS
An Imprint of W. H. Smith Publishers Inc.
112 Madison Avenue
New York City 10016

Contents ★★★★★★★★★★★

★★★★★★★★★★★★★★

POCAHONTAS (1595-1617) ★★★

The Indian Princess who charmed England

★

Pocahontas was the daughter of an Indian chief. When she was 12, she threw herself at her father's feet to plead for the life of a British colonist, Capt. John Smith, whom her tribe had captured. The old chief set the prisoner free.

In 1613, Pocahontas was taken hostage by the colonists. They taught her to speak English. They told her about their God, and Pocahontas was baptized as a Christian. She fell in love with an Englishman, Captain John Rolfe, and when she was released they were married.

Pocahontas, aged 21.

In 1616, the Rolfes sailed to England, where Pocahontas was presented to Queen Anne. Everyone was charmed by the princess. She would have been happy to stay in England, but Rolfe insisted they return to Virginia.

A few days after they sailed from London, Pocahontas became so sick that she had to be taken off the ship. She died of smallpox almost as soon as she was taken ashore. The Indian princess was buried in the crypt of a church in Gravesend, southern England.

★

Benjamin ★★★★★★★★★

FRANKLIN (1706-1790) ★★★★

The printer who drafted the Constitution

★

When Benjamin Franklin was 12, after only two years at school, he was sent to work with his brother, a printer. While he was learning his trade, he read anything he could lay his hands on and even wrote articles for his brother's newspaper, *The New England Courant*.

In 1723, Franklin went to Philadelphia, where he found a job with a small printing plant. He worked hard, and continued to read and read.

The Governor of Pennsylvania was so impressed when he met Franklin that he offered to finance his trip to England to buy printing equipment.

But when Franklin arrived in London in 1724, he discovered that his patron had let him down. He persuaded a British printer to give him a job, and within 18 months he had saved enough money to go home.

In 1729, Franklin founded the *Pennsylvania Gazette*. The paper prospered, and so did Franklin. He was elected to the colonists' assembly and held several important posts.

★

Franklin reads the first issue of the Pennsylvania Gazette *in 1729.*

Franklin experiments with lightning.

Franklin was fascinated by science. His experiments with a kite led him to identify lightning electricity, and he discovered the Gulf Stream and its course.

In 1757, he was sent to England to insist that the American Colony had the right to raise its own taxes. He went back to London in 1766 to argue the case for tax-paying colonists' right to vote.

Ten years later, Franklin was one of the men who helped draw up the Declaration of Independence, and when war broke out with Britain, he went to France to negotiate an alliance between the French and the colonists.

Franklin succeeded in his mission, and also became a great success with the ladies of Paris! Despite his years – he was over 70 by now – he became known as the most charming ladies-man in the city.

When he returned to America, he was appointed to the committee that wrote the Constitution.

On Franklin's death, George Washington, President of the new independent United States, said that America had lost, "a genius, a philosopher, a scientist, a noble statesman, and its first citizen."

George ★★★★★★★★★

WASHINGTON (1732-1799) ★★★

First President of the United States

★

George Washington

George Washington's wealthy, plantation-owning parents encouraged him to join the Virginia Militia as soon as he was old enough. He rose to the rank of lieutenant-colonel. Once, during a skirmish in 1755, four bullets ripped through his coat, but he carried on fighting.

Washington returned to his Virginian estates in 1759, but in 1774 he was elected to the Continental Congress at Philadelphia. Like many plantation owners, Washington objected to British rule, and when it became clear that war was inevitable, he was appointed Commander-in-Chief of the ill-trained Continental Army.

In 1781, with French backing, Washington forced the surrender of General Cornwallis at Yorktown, Virginia.

With independence ensured, Washington retired to Mount Vernon. But, by 1787, he and other leading figures, concerned by the near collapse of the Confederation Government, summoned the Constitution Convention at Philadelphia.

By 1788, nine states had accepted the Constitution, which provided for the election of a president voted for by representatives from the different states. On February 4, 1789, Washington was elected the first President of the United States.

The presidential mansion was a grand house on Cherry Street in New York City, where George and his wife, Martha, behaved with such formality that critics thought that the presidency had gone to Washington's head!

Washington was determined to establish the right of the Federal government to interfere in the internal affairs of individual states, and was equally determined to put down Indian resistance in the North-West Territory.

In 1793, he was re-elected for a second term, during which he insisted America remain neutral in the French Revolution. He personally commanded troops in western Pennsylvania to subdue the backwoodsmen who were violently opposed to a tax on the whiskey they distilled.

Toward the end of his first term, Washington laid the foundation stone of the White House. But he died before it was completed. He is the only president not to have lived at the White House.

Washington refused a third term in office, and withdrew to Mount Vernon, where he died in his favorite four-poster bed in 1799.

Washington at the Constitutional Convention, 1787.

Daniel

BOONE (1734-1820)

American pioneer

★

There's a statue of Daniel Boone in the National Capitol building in Washington D.C. It shows him grappling with an Indian – and that's how we think of him.

When Boone was a child, his family went to live on the North Carolina frontier. In 1755, he was one of the colonists who marched with Washington in Gen. Braddock's ill-fated army, which was defeated by Indians at the Battle of the Wilderness.

The same year, he led a group of settlers along the Wilderness Road into Kentucky. From 1769 he spent most of his time in the forest, trapping and exploring the land. He was captured by the Shawnee Indians in 1778 and held prisoner for five months until he escaped.

During his captivity, Boone learned to think like an Indian, and when the Shawnees attacked his settlement, Boonesboro, he was able to anticipate their battle tactics and win.

Stories about Boone spread East and he became a legendary trail blazer, one of the brave men who opened up America.

Daniel Boone, frontiersman.

Paul ★★★★★★★★★★★

REVERE (1735-1818) ★★★★★★

"The British are coming!"

★

By the time he was 30 years old, Paul Revere was one of the American Colony's leading silversmiths. Like many Americans he hated British rule, and he was a member of the Anti-British Society.

In 1773, Revere took part in the famous Boston Tea Party, where about 50 men, dressed as Mohawk Indians, boarded British tea ships in Boston Harbor and threw the tea into the water.

In April, 1775, when the Virginia Provincial Assembly learned Gen. Gage was planning to seize the colonists' ammunition depot and arrest leading "revolutionaries," Revere was sent to warn everyone.

Revere, War of Independence hero.

Revere rode hell for leather through the night to warn the local resistance. He covered the 16 miles from Boston to Lexington in only two hours, calling, as the story goes: "The British are coming! The British are coming!"

The following day, the War of Independence began.

In one skirmish with the British, Revere's men were forced to retreat. Revere was branded a coward.

It took Revere three years to clear his name. If he hadn't, he may not have entered history as one of America's great heroes.

Thomas ★★★★★★★★★

JEFFERSON (1743-1826) ★★★★

The man who drafted the Declaration of Independence
★

When Thomas Jefferson went to Williamsburg, Virginia, to go to college, the lanky, freckled lad with a mop of red hair, who had been brought up on his father's estate in Virginia, had never seen a town.

When he graduated in 1762 he became a lawyer, and in 1775 he became a delegate to the Second Continental Congress. A year later, he was appointed to a committee to draft the Declaration of Independence.

Jefferson held office in the Virginia State Legislature between 1776 and 1779, where he advocated the separation of church and state and the gradual abolition of slavery.

At the Confederation Congress of 1783-1784, Jefferson proposed the adoption of decimal coinage based on the dollar.

In 1790, after five years as America's ambassador to France, Jefferson became Secretary of State. But he clashed so violently with the Secretary of the Treasury over his views about the future development of the United States that he resigned in 1793.

Jefferson – 3rd President of the U.S.

Jefferson with the Declaration Committee of American Independence, 1776.

He was persuaded back into politics, becoming Vice-President in 1796 and, after a dead-heat election, President in 1801.

Jefferson's greatest achievement as President was the Louisiana Purchase of 1803. The 865,000 square miles he bought from France added the land from which more than six states were to be carved. It cost, roughly, 8 cents an acre!

While in office, Jefferson replaced the curtsies and bows, which President Washington had insisted upon, with simple handshakes. He hated being President, and was happy to retire at the end of his second term. He went to live in the country, where he cultivated the first tomatoes to grow in America, compiled recipe books and designed clocks and furniture.

Jefferson was the first American to be innoculated against smallpox and is credited with introducing ice cream, macaroni and waffles into America. Perhaps he over-indulged in these foods, because he died from an acute stomach upset in 1826.

John Paul

★★★★★★★★

JONES (1747-1792)

★★★★★★

America's first naval hero

★

When he was 12, Scots-born John Paul sailed to America as a cabin boy. Nine years later he was master of a slave ship.

On one voyage, John Paul shot a sailor. When his ship docked he laid low for a while, and added Jones to his name to escape trial.

During the War of Independence, Jones joined the American naval force and the next year captured the English ship, *Drake*.

In 1779, he achieved his greatest victory when he challenged two British warships. Just as his men boarded one of them, *Serapis*, their own ship sank!

With the war over, the naval force was disbanded and Jones offered his services to the Russians. He won many honors for his victories against the Turks.

In 1792, Jones died in France. His body lay in an unmarked grave until 1905, when it was taken back to America. It was reburied with full military honors at the U.S. Naval Academy at Annapolis, Maryland.

★

John Paul Jones, naval hero.

Betsy

ROSS (1752-1836)

She sewed the Stars and Stripes – or did she?

★

In 1776, a committee of distinguished Americans resolved that the United States' flag should consist of 13 red and white stripes, and have white stars on a blue background. They asked Betsy Ross, who made flags for the Pennsylvania State Navy, to stitch the flag for them . . .

Sadly, this story is mere legend. The resolution to adopt the Stars and Stripes was not taken until June 14, 1777.

It was not until nearly 100 years later that Ross's grandson, in a lecture to the Pennsylvania Historical Society in 1870, claimed that Ross had sewn the Stars and Stripes. Somehow, people believed him and the legend stuck.

Ross's house in Arch Street, Philadelphia, Pennsylvania, is now an historic monument, and on every Flag Day, June 14, a wreath is placed on her grave – a nice tradition commemorating historical inaccuracy!

★

Betsy Ross displays one of the American flags she manufactured.

Washington ★★★★★★★★

IRVING (1783-1859) ★★★★★★

Creator of Rip Van Winkle

★

Washington Irving had little formal schooling, but his father had a large library and the lad spent most of his time with his nose in a book.

In 1809, he published *A History of New York* under the name Diedrich Knickerbocker. The book was a huge success.

Irving went to England in 1815 and stayed for several years. The stories and travel articles that he sent back to America were eventually published as the work of Geoffrey Crayon, Gent. Included in them was *Rip Van Winkle*, the story of a lazy farmer who fell asleep for 20 years, and *The Legend of Sleepy Hollow*. Both became children's favorites.

Washington Irving, great American writer.

When Irving went to Spain as a diplomatic attaché, he wrote a biography of Christopher Columbus, which scholars still hold in high regard. He also wrote a five-volume biography of the man he had been named after, George Washington.

Washington Irving is recognized as the first American man of letters, who did so much to link American and European writing.

Davy ★★★★★★★★★★

CROCKETT (1786-1836) ★★★★

King of the wild frontier

★

During the Creek War of 1813-14, Davy Crockett was a scout for Andrew Jackson. When it was over, he was appointed Justice of the Peace for Tennessee.

In 1827, someone jokingly suggested Crockett should run for Congress. He did; and he won, becoming known as the "Coonskin Congressman," because he preferred hunting bears to politics. It's said he killed 100 grizzlies in just nine months.

In 1835, Crockett lost his seat and, "rather than sit on my butt doin' nothin," he set off for the Alamo, a fortified mission in San Antonio, Texas, where Texan soldiers were being attacked by the Mexican army.

Shortly after Crockett arrived, the Mexicans besieged the mission and after a 13-day bombardment, forced their way in. Crockett led 187 men in hand-to-hand combat against the attackers, but they were hopelessly outnumbered. Within a few hours it was all over. Crockett, and all the other Texans, had been slaughtered.

Within a few years, Davy Crockett had become a folk hero.

Crockett, the "Coonskin Congressman."

19

John ★★★★★★★★★★★
BROWN (1800-1859) ★★★★★★

His soul goes marching on

★

John Brown – hero to slaves.

John Brown's father was an active slavery abolitionist who helped to ship runaway slaves to freedom on the "underground railroad." When he was 12, Brown swore eternal war on slavery, just like his father.

At 30, Brown was a successful tanner. But the depression of 1837 wiped him out financially. Even so, he continued to hide runaway slaves.

Brown became more and more convinced that slavery could only be abolished by revolution, and in 1858 he began to recruit men and money to establish a military stronghold in Virginia as a refuge for runaway slaves.

But he needed guns, so in October 1859 Brown and his "army" attacked the armory in Harper's Ferry, Virginia. Several of his men were shot. Brown and the survivors barricaded themselves in an engine house, holding out against Gen. Lee's troops, until he was shot.

John Brown was hanged for treason, insurrection and murder on December 2, 1859 – a traitor to those who supported slavery, a hero to those who loathed it.

Nat

TURNER (1800-1831) ★★★★★★

The slave who led a revolution

★

When Nat Turner was born, his mother, a slave, had to be tied down to prevent her from killing her baby! She couldn't bear the thought of her son as a slave.

As Turner grew up, he became convinced that Christ had chosen him to lead the slaves from bondage, and when he was 30, he chose four "disciples" to help him in his mission.

The five men broke into Turner's master's house and slaughtered him, his wife and three children with a hatchet. Then the killers set off on a bloody trail across Southampton County, Virginia, savagely killing white slave-owners and their families and picking up recruits, until their ranks had swollen to 60.

Eventually, Turner was captured and hanged in a town called Jerusalem.

Although Turner was an unsavory character, his rebellion led a nationwide debate on the morality of slavery, which ended in its abolition later that century.

Turner – born a slave, died in captivity.

Gen. Robert E.

LEE (1807-1870)

The South's Civil War hero

★

Robert Edward Lee came from a wealthy family, owning large tracts of land in Virginia. His father was a Revolutionary general who was nicknamed Light-Horse Harry.

Shortly after Lee graduated from military academy, he married and settled in a large house on the Potomac, across from the White House.

He was severely wounded during the Mexican War (1846-1848), and when it was over he took command of the U.S. Military Academy. Later, he was posted to Texas.

When John Brown made his famous arms raid on Harper's Ferry, it was Lee's men who captured him. Lee was recalled to Washington in 1861 when the southern states broke from the Union. But he was loyal to the breakaway state Virginia. He resigned from the army and two days later was appointed commander of the Virginia forces.

Gen. Robert E. Lee

He was a brilliant military tactician and was idolized by his men. He routed the Union army in a seven-day series of battles in defense of Richmond, Virginia. In 1862, he won the second Battle of Bull Run – a shattering defeat for the Union army.

Eventually, Lee was defeated at the Battle of Gettysburg. It was the turning point of the Civil War. The Unionists were on their way to victory.

From 1864 to 1865, Lee was pitted against Gen. Grant's much larger army, which took Petersburg in April 1865. When Grant's troops captured Richmond a few days later, Lee recognized defeat was inevitable. He surrendered – with tears in his eyes.

After the war, Lee became President of Washington College. The year after his death it was renamed the Washington and Lee University, in honor of one of our greatest soldiers.

Gen. Lee (seated) with his staff, in 1865.

Abraham

LINCOLN (1809-1865)

From log cabin to the White House

★

Shortly after Abraham Lincoln was born, he was given to a cousin to hold. "He'll never come to much," said the lad.

Young Lincoln was educated at local schools, and when he wasn't helping his father on the land, he was reading books. He grew taller and taller until he stood at 6′ 4″ and was as strong as an ox.

After his family settled in Illinois, Lincoln was elected to the state government in 1833. Thirteen years later, as a successful lawyer, he was elected to Congress. He decided not to stand for re-election in 1849.

Then it was suggested that Nebraska be admitted to the Union as two states, Nebraska and Kansas. Kansas was to be a slave state and Nebraska a free one. This outraged anti-slavers, including Lincoln, and they campaigned long and loud against the Bill.

By 1860, Lincoln's eloquent stand against slavery had made him so famous that the Republican party selected him as their presidential candidate. He was eventually inaugurated as President in 1861.

Lincoln – 16th President of the U.S.

John Wilkes Booth shoots Lincoln at the theater, April 14, 1865.

In his inaugural address, President Lincoln said he would not interfere with slavery where it already existed, but no new slave states would be created and the Union was to be indissoluble. Shortly after Lincoln's election, the Civil War began.

Even Lincoln's political enemies admired his humor, patience, brilliant speeches and his courage. His height made him stand out among others, and he added to it by always wearing a battered top hat, inside which he often carried important state papers.

On January 1, 1863, Lincoln proclaimed emancipation for all slaves. In 1864 he was re-elected President, and the next year Robert E. Lee surrendered his army. The war was virtually over.

On April 14, 1865, Lincoln and his wife were at the theater in Washington. A fanatical southerner, John Wilkes Booth, slipped into Lincoln's box and shot him.

The man who emancipated slaves and led the North to victory in the War died the next morning. "Now," said the Secretary for War, "he belongs to the Ages."

UNCLE SAM . . .

. . . Born on the fourth of July

In the early days of the 19th century, Elbert Anderson owned a small store in Troy, New York, which was tended by his cousin, Ebenezer, and his uncle, Samuel Wilson, who was known to everyone as "Uncle Sam."

Elbert Anderson was a fervent patriot, and alongside his own name on the storefront he had written "U.S."

"What's that for?" one of the store clerks asked Sam one day.

"That's me," said Sam. "Uncle Sam: United States. Same thing."

The joke spread around Troy and, later, throughout the country. Within a few years, "Uncle Sam" had caught on as the symbol of the United States. His famous Stars and Stripes coat and pants originally belonged to a cartoon character called Major Jack Downing, who was popular at the time when "Uncle Sam" Wilson cracked his joke.

I WANT YOU
FOR U.S. ARMY
NEAREST RECRUITING STATION

★

Uncle Sam later featured on U.S. army recruitment posters during World War I (1914-1918).

Susan B. ★★★★★★★★

ANTHONY (1820-1906) ★★★★★

Social reformer and early feminist

★

Susan Brownell Anthony, born into a Quaker family, could read and write by the time she was three years old.

When she was six, her family moved from Massachusetts to Battensville, New York, and it was there that Susan saw a black man for the first time. She was terrified, but when she learned that black men and women were bought and sold like cattle her opinion changed.

After a strict Quaker upbringing, Anthony became one of the leading social reformers of her time. She organized the Women's State Temperence Society of New York, campaigned against slavery and advocated women should have the vote. She was fined $100 for voting in elections when it was illegal for women to do so. But she refused to pay.

Anthony has been the only woman to be honored by having her imprint on a coin – the Anthony silver dollar. It caused an uproar at the time.

During her campaigns Anthony was pelted with rotten eggs, hissed at and criticized in the Press. But once she had taken up a cause, nothing would shake her belief in it. By the time she died she was one of the most respected women in America.

Susan B. Anthony, anti-slave campaigner.

Gen. William T. SHERMAN (1820-1891)

★★★★★
★★★★★

The North's Civil War hero

★

By 1853, William Tecumseh Sherman, who graduated from the U.S. Military Academy in 1840, resigned from the army to work in a bank. But when the Civil War started in 1861, he became a colonel in the Unionist infantry.

Sherman was promoted after the Battle of Bull Run, but when he asked for 200,000 men to take Kentucky for the North, his superiors thought he was crazy and stripped him of his command. However, he soon had his own division again.

He fought at Shiloh, and in 1863 drove General Johnston out of Jackson, Mississippi. In 1864, Sherman evacuated Atlanta, Georgia, and ordered that the city be burned. After giving his men a short rest, he marched them 300 miles to Savannah, Georgia, to take the city for the North.

Sherman's men worshipped him. Their "Uncle Billy" lived rough, like they did. He inspired their confidence. "There's Uncle Billy," they would say. "All's right."

★

Gen. Sherman, Civil War hero.

Clara ★★★★★★★★★
BARTON (1821-1912) ★★★★★★

Founder of the American Red Cross

★

Clara Barton was a humble clerk in the U.S. Patent Office, but when the Civil War started she rounded up as many girlfriends as she could and organized a volunteer service to tend the wounded.

In 1865, Lincoln asked Barton to take charge of the letters that were flooding in from all over America asking about missing soldiers. With a small team, she traveled all over the country trying to identify unmarked graves.

In 1869, she went to Switzerland to attend the International Red Cross convention, and a year later she was back at the battlefront, comforting sick soldiers during the Franco-Prussian War.

Barton campaigned long and hard to have America accepted into the International Red Cross Organization. It took her almost 12 years of bullying to win international recognition for her American Red Cross. It was Barton who made sure that whenever disaster of any kind struck, the Red Cross was there.

★

Clara Barton of the American Red Cross.

Harriet

TUBMAN (1821-1913)

The slaves' Moses

★

When she was a child slave, Harriet Tubman so angered a slave overseer that he smashed her skull. Tubman survived, but from then on she fell asleep several times a day and, when she awoke, would carry on the conversation at precisely the point where she had nodded off!

Everyone thought Tubman was half-witted. She wasn't. In 1849, she escaped to the North where she dedicated herself to struggle for the complete emancipation of her people.

Day and night, Tubman worked as a domestic, and whenever she had saved enough money she would slip back to the South at enormous danger to herself, and lead out groups of escaped slaves.

Tubman was ruthless. Once, when a slave collapsed, exhausted, saying he couldn't go on, Tubman pointed her revolver at him and said, "You go or die. Dead niggers tell no tales."

By the time Tubman made her last trip in 1860, she had led more than 300 slaves to freedom.

★

Tubman was nurse, scout and spy for the Federal army during the Civil War.

Gen. Ulysses S.

GRANT (1822-1885)

Civil War hero and two-term President

★

When 2nd lieutenant "Sam" Grant was fighting in the Mexican War, a fellow officer, Robert E. Lee, noted that he behaved with "distinction and gallantry."

When the Civil War broke out, Grant was appointed Colonel of an Illinois Unionist regiment. He was such a brilliant soldier that, within three years, he was Commander of the Union Armies, and it was to Grant that his old major in the Mexican War, Lee, surrendered in 1865.

Three years later, Grant was elected President. During his first term, America went through a period of such prosperity that Grant was elected for a second term in 1872. He was a scrupulously honest man, but his administration was one of the most corrupt on record.

When Grant retired his business went bankrupt, and in order to make money, he started writing his memoirs. He finished them four days before he died of cancer. When the book was published, it made $500,000 for his widow and his children.

Gen. Grant – 18th President of the U.S.

"Stonewall"

JACKSON (1824-1863)

Great Confederate general

Thomas Jackson proved that he was a capable soldier during the Mexican War (1846-1848). At the outbreak of the Civil War in 1861, he was given command of a Confederate brigade. At the first Battle of Bull Run he stood his ground, according to a fellow officer, "like a stone wall." Thereafter, he was known as "Stonewall" Jackson.

During the Shenandoah campaign, Jackson defeated three Union generals. In September 1862, he took 13,000 prisoners at Harper's Ferry and the next day his troops saved the day for General Lee at Antietam.

Then a lieutenant-general, Jackson commanded the right wing of the southern army at Fredericksburg, Virginia. At the Battle of Chancellorsville, in Virginia, he repulsed General Hooker's men, but the next night, when returning from an inspection between the lines, he was shot by his own men who mistook his party for Union spies. He died shortly afterward. His men wept openly when they heard Jackson was dead.

Gen. "Stonewall" Jackson

GERONIMO (1829-1909) ★★★★

Indian chief

★

When the first pioneers began to move westward, they had to travel through Indian territory and settle in lands that had been Indian for centuries. The settlers' wagon trains and farms were constantly attacked by bands of Indians, who killed men, women and children.

The south-west of the country was Apache territory, and one of their most feared leaders was Geronimo. He was a brilliant military commander who led his men in attack after attack against the settlers. Even after his people were captured and forced to settle on a barren reserve in Arizona, the Indians carried on the battle.

In 1886, Geronimo surrendered to the U.S. Cavalry. It was agreed that the Indians be allowed to settle in Florida. But, instead, they were imprisoned! They were eventually settled in Oklahoma where Geronimo died, a hero to his braves and still feared by the white men who cheated him.

★

Geronimo, brave Indian warrior.

Mark

TWAIN (1835-1910)

Author of *Tom Sawyer* and *Huckleberry Finn*

★

Samuel Clemens, alias Mark Twain.

At the age of 12, Samuel Langhorne Clemens was a trainee printer on a local newspaper in Missouri. In 1857, he became an apprentice riverboat pilot on the Mississippi River. He often heard the pilots calling the words, "mark twain," meaning the depth of the water was two fathoms (12 feet).

The Civil War put an end to Mississippi river boating. Clemens became a journalist, and chose the pen name Mark Twain.

In 1865, his story, *The Celebrated Jumping Frog of Claveras County*, established him as a top humorist, and 11 years later, *The Adventures of Tom Sawyer*, based on his own boyhood, became a best seller. This was followed by *The Adventures of Huckleberry Finn* – a comic study of racial problems.

One of the most famous stories told about Mark Twain is that, one day, he read his own obituary in a newspaper. He immediately cabled Associated Press with the immortal words: "The report of my death was an exaggeration."

Admiral George

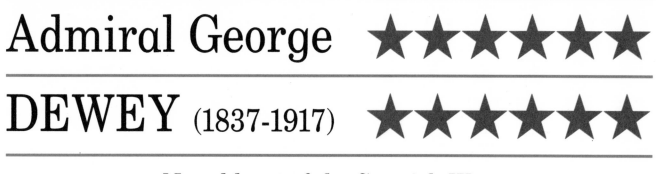

DEWEY (1837-1917)

Naval hero of the Spanish War

★

By 1898 George Dewey had worked his way up from student at the U.S. Naval Academy, to the rank of Commodore. In that year, the Spanish Navy sank a U.S. battleship in Havana harbor and two months later America and Spain were at war.

Dewey, who was in command of the U.S. Asiatic squadron (four cruisers and two gunboats), was given secret orders to sail from Hong Kong to the Philippines and engage the Spanish fleet which was at anchor in Manila harbor.

Dewey's ships sailed into Manila Bay on April 30. At 5.40 the next morning, the battle started. By noon, all 10 of the Spanish ships had been destroyed. Only eight American sailors had been wounded.

The victory made America a major Pacific power, and when Dewey sailed home he was hailed a hero and presented with the Sword of Honor by Congress.

★

Dewey as Commodore of the U.S. Navy.

"Wild Bill"

★★★★★★★★★

HICKOK (1837-1876) ★★★★★★

Soldier, scout and U.S. Marshal

★

James Butler Hickok was reckoned to be one of the best shots in Illinois. When he was a stagecoach driver on the Santa Fe Trail, he killed a bear with his bowie knife. When he was on the overland stage he killed the leader and two other members of the notorious McCanles Gang.

During the Civil War, Hickok was a spy for the Union Army. He was captured several times and sentenced to be shot, but he always escaped.

Hickok became Deputy Marshal and Marshal of three of the roughest towns in the Wild West and also fought with Generals Hancock, Sheridan and Custer in their battles against frontier Indians.

"Wild Bill" Hickok, the gentle giant.

Despite his tough reputation, Hickok was a quiet, mild-mannered man who never killed a single man other than in self-defense or in the line of duty.

Hickok was murdered in 1876, and is buried in the cemetry in Deadwood, South Dakota.

Gen. George

CUSTER (1839-1876) ★★★★★★

The soldier who made a "last stand"

★

George Armstrong Custer was brave, handsome and dashing with shoulder-length red hair cascading from under his cap. But he was a boastful braggard, desperate for glory, and was a disaster as a soldier.

After the Battle of Gettysburg, where he led a successful but foolish Cavalry charge, he was constantly in disgrace. Once, he lost some of his men on a march and simply abandoned them. He was officially disgraced for shooting deserters, and he was a ruthless killer of innocent Cheyenne women.

In 1876, Custer and his troops were camped near the Little Big Horn River in Montana. Custer's commander told him to stay at his post, but, as usual, Custer thought he knew better. Without knowing how many Indians were on the other side or even scouting the land, he decided to charge across the river.

Even before he crossed the river he was totally surrounded by Indians. He and his men made their famous last stand, but the Indians had little difficulty in wiping out Custer and his troops.

Gen. George A. Custer

John D. ROCKERFELLER (1839-1937)

The richest man in the world

★

John Davison Rockerfeller started work as an office clerk when he was 16. Then he started up his own business, and by 1865, he had made more than enough money to go into partnership with oil man Samuel Andrews.

The company quickly became the leading oil firm in Cleveland, Ohio, and in 1870 Rockerfeller, Andrews and their associates raised $1 million to start The Standard Oil Company. Within 10 years, it controlled 90 per cent of U.S. oil refineries and had made its owners vast fortunes.

John D. Rockerfeller

Standard Oil became so powerful and had such a strangle hold on the oil business that, in 1911, the Supreme Court ordered it be closed. The company's case was not helped when some of their underhand business methods became public. But, by that time, Rockerfeller was the richest man in the world.

During his life, Rockerfeller gave away $500 million to charities, as well as to science, education and public health. By the time he died, he was one of the most popular men in America.

William "Buffalo Bill" ★★★
CODY (1846-1917) ★★★★★★★

The man who took the Wild West to Europe

★

When Bill Cody was 14, he joined the famous Pony Express, spending several years carrying mail through dangerous Indian territory.

During the Civil War, Cody scouted for the Cavalry against the Indians. He became a hero when he killed Yellowhand, the Cheyenne chief, in one-to-one combat.

When the war was over, Cody won the contract to supply meat to the Kansas Pacific Railway, and in 18 months he killed 4,280 buffaloes – single-handed!

"Buffalo Bill" of the Wild West.

Cody then turned to show business. He starred in a revue called *The Scouts of the Prairie* before producing his own production, *Buffalo Bill's Wild West Show*, a huge success. The show had Indians, cowboys, rough-riders and crack-shooters. After thrilling audiences all over America, he took the show to Europe, where people flocked to see the rip-roaring spectacle.

Sadly, *Buffalo Bill's Wild West Show* ran into financial difficulties and Cody, one of America's greatest showmen, retired. He occasionally returned to appear in other people's shows, but mainly he spent his time writing – what else? – Wild West novels.

Alexander Graham

BELL (1847-1922)

The man who invented the telephone

Alexander Graham Bell was born in Edinburgh, Scotland, but emigrated to Canada and then to Boston. In 1871, he became Professor of Vocal Physiology, having devoted his life to teaching the deaf.

One day, Bell read in a scientific journal that a German scientist had invented a way of transmitting the human voice using electricity. He began to learn about electricity, so he could try his own experiments.

In 1874, Bell met a businessman who offered to finance Bell's experiments. Within two years, he had devised a machine that could transmit the human voice. In 1876, his assistant picked up the receiver and heard Bell's voice crackle: "Mr. Watson. Come here, I want you." It wasn't too long before telephones were being installed in offices and homes.

In fact, Bell had misread the original scientific report. The German scientist had not actually invented a telephone. Bell's was the first!

Alexander Graham Bell in 1876, the year when the telephone first "spoke."

Joseph PULITZER (1847-1911)

Newspaper magnate and founder of the Pulitzer Prize

★

Joseph Pulitzer left his native Hungary in 1864 to enlist in the U.S. Army. He was discharged a year later, and made his way to St. Louis, Missouri, to make his fortune. He was penniless when he arrived there, but got a job as a newspaper reporter. By 1880, he was the proud owner of the St. Louis *Post-Dispatch*.

In 1883, Pulitzer bought the New York *World*. The circulation battle with its rival, *The Journal*, led to both papers printing stories which were sensational and lurid, in order to attract the readers. This dirty battle gave rise to the phrase "Yellow Journalism."

Pulitzer later changed the editorial policy of his paper and it became one of the most respected papers in America.

In 1903, Pulitzer announced he was giving a fortune to found the Columbia School of Journalism. Part of this money was to be used to establish prizes for outstanding achievements in the arts. Seven years after Joseph Pulitzer's death, the first of many Pulitzer Prizes were awarded.

Pulitzer – journalist and benefactor.

Thomas Alva

★★★★★★★

EDISON (1847-1931)

★★★★★★

America's most prolific inventor

★

Thomas Alva Edison

Thomas Alva Edison only received three months' proper schooling. By the time he was 12, he was earning money by selling newspapers on a train. He was also interested in chemistry, and carried out simple experiments in his spare time.

Eventually, Edison saved enough money to buy the sole rights to sell newspapers on the railroad line. He bought some printing equipment and founded the *The Grand Trunk Herald*, actually printing it on a train. While the paper was printing, Edison would be experimenting in the baggage car.

Edison turned his attention to full-time inventing, and by the time he died he had taken out patents for hundreds of ideas, including a sewing machine powered by the human voice, and of course, his two most famous inventions, the light bulb and the phonograph.

Edison demonstrated the first electric light bulb in 1879. Two years before, he had invented the phonograph, the ancestor of today's record player and compact disc.

Booker T. ★★★★★★★★

WASHINGTON (1856-1915) ★★★

The slave who became an educator and reformer

★

Booker Taliaferro Washington was born a slave. As a child, he worked in the mines by day and went to school at night. He was so keen to be educated that, in 1872, he walked 300 miles to go to college, where he worked as a janitor to pay his way. When he graduated, he taught school and studied law.

In 1881, Washington went to Tuskagee, Alabama, to found a school for blacks. He had to start from scratch, because there weren't even plans for a building. Within a year, he had raised enough money to get the school under way.

The excellence of the Tuskagee Institute became well known and Booker's outspoken attacks on racial inequality, violence and the economic exploitation of blacks brought him widespread fame.

Harvard University awarded Washington an honorary Masters of Arts degree in 1896 and Dartmouth College conferred the Doctor of Laws degree on him. By the time he died he was the most respected and most famous black southerner of his generation.

★

Booker T. Washington

43

Woodrow ★★★★★★★★★
WILSON (1856-1924) ★★★★★★

The President who won the Nobel peace prize

★

Thomas Woodrow Wilson, the son of a Presbyterian minister, suffered from dyslexia, which meant he had great trouble reading. But that didn't stop him studying law, politics and history, and eventually becoming President of Princeton University.

Wilson's talent for organizing and his modern thinking brought him to the attention of the New Jersey Democratic Party bosses, who persuaded him to stand for governor. They hoped if he was elected, they would be able to control him. He was elected; and they couldn't.

The reforms Wilson advocated made him so popular that when the Democrats were looking for a presidential candidate in 1912, they decided (on the 46th ballot) Wilson was their man.

During his two-term presidency (he was re-elected in 1916) Wilson instituted several important economic reforms, including the Farm Loan scheme, which enabled farmers to take out long-term, low-interest loans. His administration also recognized trades unions' right to strike.

★

Wilson – 28th President of the U.S.

President Wilson with his second wife, Edith Grant.

When he was President, Congress passed the 18th Amendment, prohibiting the sale of intoxicating liquor in the United States. Prohibition became very unpopular, and many gangsters became rich and powerful by supplying illegal liquor.

When Europe went to war in 1914, Wilson kept his country out of the conflict until 1917, when an intercepted telegram from Germany to Mexico promised that parts of Texas, New Mexico and Arizona would be returned to Mexico if she declared war on America!

In 1918, Wilson suggested that when the War was over "a general association of nations to keep the peace in future" be established. The Peace Treaty of Versailles allowed for just such a body – The League of Nations – and Wilson was awarded the Nobel peace prize in 1919.

Annie

OAKLEY (1860-1926)

The woman who couldn't miss

★

When Phoebe Anne Oakley Moses was just six years old, she was already shooting rabbits in the woods surrounding her family's log cabin in Darke County, Ohio.

In her teens, Oakley outshot Frank Butler, a famous marksman, in a Cincinatti shoot-out. A few years later she married him, and the husband-and-wife team toured the country in circuses before joining Buffalo Bill's *Wild West Show* as star sharp-shooters.

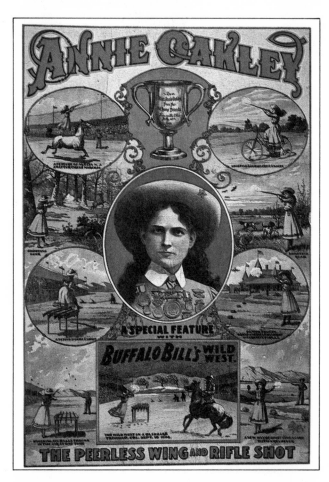

Oakley's skill was amazing. She could hit a coin tossed in the air 90 feet away, and when she was in Berlin, Germany, she shot a cigarette from Kaiser Willhelm's lips! "I had to get that one," she said, "else they'd've gotten me!"

Oakley died unbeaten in any shooting match, but her name lives on. Nowadays, a free ticket to a show will have a hole punched in it. These tickets are called *Annie Oakleys.*

★

Annie Oakley featured on many posters advertising "Buffalo Bill" Cody's Wild West Show. *She was billed as "The Peerles Wing and Rifle Shot."*

Anna Mary "Grandma" ★★★
MOSES (1860-1961) ★★★★★★

America's grand old lady of painting

★

Like many farming women, "Grandma" Moses spent the long New York state winter evenings embroidering yarn pictures. She later turned to painting, but when she exhibited her pictures at the local fairs, she won no prizes for them. Her jam and canned fruits, though, won several awards!

Then Lũis Caldor, an art collector, bought three of "Grandma" Moses' works and exhibited them at the Museum of Modern Art in New York. Suddenly her simple "primitive" paintings were in demand. The colorful, detailed country landscapes remembered from her childhood, dotted with characters in period costume, were irresistible works of art.

"Grandma" Moses died aged 101 years!

In 1940, when "Grandma" Moses was 80, she was given her first one-woman show, which she called *What a Farmwife Painted*. It was an instant success. She became famous overnight.

"Grandma" Moses carried on painting almost to the end of her life, and today her works hang in many important art galleries.

Henry

★★★★★★★★★★

FORD (1863-1947) ★★★★★★★

The man who built an automobile for the nation

★

In the early days of this century, only the rich could afford automobiles. Henry Ford was the man who changed all that.

He worked on his father's farm until, at 17, he got a job in a machine shop in Detroit, Michigan, for $2.50 a week.

Ford spent his spare time on the farm making steam tractors and in 1896, after a spell as Chief Engineer with the Edison Company, he produced his first automobile.

He was quick to see the advantages of assembly-line production, and in 1908, the first mass-produced Ford – the Model T – rolled out of his factory. By 1925, 10,000 Fords were being produced every day. Within 28 years of the first Model T, there were more than 15 million on the roads.

Although the assembly line was completely streamlined for efficiency, Ford gave his early customers some choice. "They can have any color they want," he said, " . . . as long as it's black!"

★

Ford – father of the popular car.

William Randolph ★★★★★
HEARST (1863-1951) ★★★★★★

The man who made the news sensational

★

William Randolph Hearst's family was enormously wealthy, and when he left Harvard he took charge of the *San Francisco Examiner*, which his father owned.

Over the next 40 years, Hearst created the biggest newspaper empire the world had ever seen, with papers in every part of America. He used every gimmick to build up circulation – banner headlines, color cartoons, sensational, often inaccurate, scoops. He even had pictures falsified to stir up public opinion, pushing America into war with Spain in 1898.

Hearst controlled all his enterprises from his extraordinary estate at San Simeon in California. It housed one of the world's largest art collections. In its grounds stood Spanish castles, which had been dismantled in Spain and carefully rebuilt in California! Today, the house is home of the Hearst Museum, containing the collection.

Hearst sometimes manipulated the truth to sell newspapers, but he was, in fact, a talented journalist and businessman.

William Randolph Hearst

Wilbur WRIGHT (1867-1912)

Orville WRIGHT (1871-1948)

Pioneers of flight

★

In 1892, Orville and Wilbur Wright opened a bicycle store in Ohio. The brothers were interested in air flight, and although men had already flown in balloons and airships, the Wrights believed that flight in a *heavier than air*, machine-powered aircraft was possible.

With the money they were making from their store, the Wright brothers started to build kites and gliders. They designed hundreds, each an improvement on the one before, and endlessly researched into wing structure, until they built a glider with which they were completely satisfied. Then they made their own aircraft engine.

Wilbur (left) and Orville (right) Wright

In December 1903, at Kitty Hawk, North Carolina, the brothers flipped a coin to decide which of them should be the first to "fly" in their machine-powered aircraft. Wilbur won . . . but the machine didn't leave the ground.

The brothers spent the rest of that day trying to find out what had gone wrong, and on December 17, with Orville at the controls, they tried again. The engine spluttered, the airplane gathered speed and took off into the air. It landed 12 seconds later. The Wright brothers had become the first men to achieve true flight.

Frank Lloyd ★★★★★★★

WRIGHT (1869-1959) ★★★★★★

America's greatest architect

★

Visitors to New York often ask what the curious spiral-shaped concrete building on the Upper East Side is. It's the Guggenheim Museum building, the work of America's most revolutionary architect, Frank Lloyd Wright.

Wright studied architecture at the University of Wisconsin. The collapse of a newly-built wing there made Wright realize you must apply engineering principles to architecture – if your buildings are going to stay upright! His buildings were not only soundly constructed but blended in with their surroundings. They were spacious and sparsely decorated.

Frank Lloyd Wright stands in front of the Guggenheim Museum, New York City.

During his 72-year career Wright designed more than 300 projects, including one house built over a waterfall in Pennsylvania. He also designed the Tokyo Imperial Hotel. When an earthquake destroyed Tokyo in 1923, the hotel was one of the few buildings that survived.

Even at the end of his life, Wright's head was full of revolutionary ideas. When he was over 80, he designed what would have been the tallest building in the world – a skyscraper, one mile high with atomic powered elevators. Sadly, it was never built.

COOLIDGE (1872-1933)

The President who said as little as possible

★

Calvin Coolidge, who was proud of the Indian blood running through his veins, came from a long line of men who had held small-time public offices, so it was not surprising that, when he became a lawyer in Massachusetts in 1897, he set out to make a career in politics.

He became a city councillor in 1908 in Northampton, Massachusetts; then a member of the State House of Representatives, mayor of Boston and eventually governor. Coolidge came to national prominence during the 1919 Boston police strike, when he refused to negotiate with the strikers and the State militia had to be called in to restore law and order.

Coolidge was Harding's running mate in the 1920 presidential election. Harding won. Coolidge became Vice-President.

When Harding died of a heart attack in 1923, Vice-President Calvin Coolidge was away from Washington, visiting his boyhood home. As soon as they heard the news, Coolidge's father, a public official, solemnly swore in his son as the 30th President of the United States.

Coolidge – 30th President of the U.S.

Coolidge is sworn in as President by his father in August 1923.

Coolidge's philosophy was: "The business of America is business," and under his administration, business boomed as it never had before. Vast fortunes were made on the stock market. (His Secretary of the Treasury is said to have made $300 million.) Of course, the prosperity did not last, but by the time of the Wall Street Crash in 1929, Coolidge was no longer President.

Coolidge's unwillingness to talk was legendary. On one occasion, when a talkative lady dinner guest said to him, "Mr. President, I have a bet that I can make you say at least three words during dinner," Coolidge turned to her and said, "You lose!" He remained silent for the rest of the meal!

Tom

SAWYER (b. 1876)

America's best-known schoolboy

★

Tom Sawyer, the hero of Mark Twain's famous novel, lived with his Bible-fearin' Aunt Polly. She was very kind to him, for "he's my own dead sister's boy" and she "ain't got the heart to lash him."

Aunt Polly had a house in the Mississippi village of St. Petersburg, where Tom became best friends with Huckleberry Finn, son of the local drunk.

Tom envied Huck because of his complete freedom to come and go as he chose, even to sleep rough whenever he felt like it, and although Tom tried, he could never spit as far as Huck.

Tom Sawyer and Huck Finn whitewash the fence – from The Adventures of Tom Sawyer.

Tom, Huck and another school friend fled in terror one night after they witnessed a murder in the local churchyard. They were so scared, they hid for days on an island in the river. By the time they plucked up the courage to go home, the townsfolk were convinced the boys had fallen in the river and drowned. When they returned, they were able to identify the murderer.

There have been boys like Tom Sawyer, but none of them have been so devious and yet so downright honest.

★

George M. COHAN (1878-1942)

Broadway's Yankee Doodle Dandy

★

In the 1880s, one of the most popular vaudeville acts in America was the Four Cohans – Ma and Pa Cohan, their daughter, and son George.

By the time Cohan was 15, he was writing scripts and gags, not only for the family's act, but for other performers as well. When he was 23, his first full-length play was produced on Broadway.

Cohan soon built up a reputation as a fine actor and playwright, but never lost sight of his beginnings as a song-and-dance man. One of his best-known creations was *Yankee Doodle Dandy*, the star-spangled figure who entertained audiences all over the country.

In 1911, Cohan opened his own theater and became a very successful manager. He was so famous, a few years after he died a statue of him was erected in Duffy Square, New York City, gazing up along Broadway, the street he helped make the theater-center of the world.

★

George M. Cohan, the star-spangled dandy.

Helen

★★★★★★★★★★★

KELLER (1880-1968) ★★★★★★

The girl who overcame blindness and deafness and inspired millions

★

Helen Keller was born in 1880 into a wealthy Alabama family. She was a healthy, happy baby but just after she had started to say her first words, she became very sick and lost the use of her eyes and ears.

Helen became so willful and destructive that some of her relatives wanted to send her to a lunatic asylum. But her father wrote to The Perkins Institute for the Blind in Boston, asking for guidance. The Institute sent Anne Sullivan to Alabama to become Helen's teacher.

When Sullivan was 14, she had been admitted to The Perkins Institute where she learned to "talk" to blind people by making signs on their hands.

The first thing Helen did when she met Sullivan was rummage through her baggage for something to eat. Then she kicked her new teacher, hard.

But very slowly, the child began to trust Sullivan, and within months Helen was connecting the signs made on her hands with objects she touched. Suddenly, Helen's world blossomed.

Helen learned new words by the hundreds, and was soon able to read using words which had been printed in raised letters.

Helen Keller as a young girl.

How the blind see: Helen "reads" her teacher Anne Sullivan's lips.

Helen Keller and her teacher became very well known. They met President Cleveland at the White House, and Alexander Graham Bell, a friend of her father.

In 1893, Keller wrote *My Story* for a magazine, and her fame spread. In 1899, she passed the entrance exam for Radcliffe College and graduated, with honors, in 1904. By this time, many of the articles she had written had been published in a book called *The Story of My Life*, and soon everyone in America was talking about this remarkable woman.

She became so famous that a film of her life was made in 1918. When she was in Britain, Helen met King George V and his wife, Queen Mary. During World War II she spent a great deal of time visiting wounded soldiers in military hospitals, and after the war she traveled all over the world. Everywhere she went, people were inspired by the wonderful way she had overcome her handicaps.

When she was 75, Keller received an honorary degree from Harvard University, the first woman to do so. A few years later, in 1961, she had become so frail that she had to retire from public life.

Keller died in 1968, having been acclaimed as one of the most inspiring women of all time.

Gen. Douglas

★★★★★★★★

MacARTHUR (1880-1964)

★★★★

One of the greatest military leaders

★

Douglas MacArthur's father was a lieutenant-general in the army, so it was no surprise when Douglas chose a military career. It was the right choice – he was decorated 13 times during World War I alone.

In 1935, having been Superintendent of the U.S. Military Academy, MacArthur became head of the U.S. Military Mission in the Philippines. After the islands' capture by Japan, MacArthur became Supreme Commander of U.S. Forces in the South-West Pacific. He recaptured the islands by a series of brilliant military tactics in 1945, and accepted the surrender of Japan later that year.

Gen. MacArthur as Commander of the United Nations Forces in Korea, 1950.

From 1945-1951 MacArthur was Supreme Commander of the Allied powers that occupied Japan. He introduced sweeping reforms that laid the foundations for Japan's future.

At the outbreak of the Korean War, MacArthur was given command of United Nations forces. But he was dismissed by President Truman for political reasons. MacArthur returned home officially in disgrace, but the American people gave him a hero's welcome.

58

Gen. MacArthur inspects the scene on his return to the Philippines in 1944 during World War II.

Franklin D. ★★★★★★★

ROOSEVELT (1882-1945) ★★★

Four-term President of the United States

★

Critics claim the only reason Franklin Delano Roosevelt, a distant cousin of President Theodore Roosevelt, won election to the New York State Senate in 1910 was that he campaigned in an automobile.

In 1912, Roosevelt campaigned for Woodrow Wilson, who appointed him Secretary of the Navy. When Alfred Smith won the Democratic nomination in 1920, he asked Roosevelt to be his vice-presidential candidate.

Their defeat was not nearly such a big blow as the infantile paralysis that struck him in 1921, leaving Roosevelt partially crippled for the rest of his life.

Roosevelt's handicap did nothing to deter him. In 1928, he was elected Governor of New York and was re-elected two years later with the largest majority in history.

In 1932, in the midst of the Great Depression, Roosevelt was chosen as the Democratic Party presidential candidate. He pledged himself to a "New Deal" for the American people, to restore prosperity to the country.

Roosevelt – 32nd President of the U.S.

Roosevelt (in the truck) at the Casablanca Conference ceremonies, 1943, where President Roosevelt met British Prime Minister Winston Churchill to discuss plans for North Africa during World War II.

During his first 100 days in office, Roosevelt spoke to the American people on the radio, explaining the sweeping reforms he had put before Congress.

His "New Deal" boosted the economy, introduced pensions, public health reforms and legislation for maximum working hours and minimum wages.

Although the Depression did not end overnight, Roosevelt was re-elected in 1936 and again in 1940. Even then, unemployment stood at 7 million. It didn't come down until the nation began to mobilize for World War II.

In 1941, Roosevelt launched a program to give the Allies in Europe "All Aid Short of War." When Japan attacked the American Fleet in Pearl Harbor, America became involved in a world-wide war to defeat Germany, Italy and Japan.

In 1943, Roosevelt visited American troops in Sicily.

In 1945, he met with the British and Russian leaders, Winston Churchill and Joseph Stalin, to discuss policies for the post-war world at the famous Yalta Conference.

Later that year, a few months before the Germans surrendered, Roosevelt was posing for an official portrait when he died.

Harry S.

TRUMAN (1884-1972)

33rd President

★

Harry Truman was born in Missouri and after High School and a variety of jobs, he worked on the family farm.

During World War I, Truman fought in France with great distinction. Almost as soon as he was back in America he married his childhood sweetheart, and opened a store in Kansas City. It went bankrupt and it took the Trumans 15 years of scrimping and saving to pay off their debts.

Truman was elected a judge in Kansas City in 1922, but he was so honest that the powerful anti-black organization, the Ku Klux Klan, made sure he wasn't re-elected.

Twenty two years later, with a distinguished reputation behind him, he became Vice-President, and when President Roosevelt suddenly died, in April 1945, he found himself President.

Nobody quite believed that the "failed haberdasher" from Kansas had the makings of a tough president. But one of Truman's first decisions was to drop the atomic bomb on Japan to end World War II. And when railroad workers went on strike, he threatened to draft them all into the army.

Harry Truman – 33rd President of the U.S.

Senator Truman (left) meets President Roosevelt at the White House after his nomination as Vice-Presidential candidate in 1944. Truman became President just months after this, when Roosevelt died suddenly in April 1945.

The man in the White House came to be highly regarded.

But Truman couldn't get his social legislation through Congress, and politicians began to write him off as a failure. In the 1948 election, he traveled 32,000 miles in 15 days, fighting a brilliant campaign, and was duly elected to the White House.

The post-war Russian domination of eastern Europe was seen by America as a huge threat to world peace. To counteract their influence Truman authorized the Marshall Plan, which pumped $3 billion into western Europe to rebuild the war-damaged economies.

During Truman's presidency, American troops fought Communism in Korea, while American politicians fought Communism at home with the famous McCarthy trials. Truman was bitterly opposed to the trials, but powerless to stop them.

Truman did not seek renomination for the 1952 election, and when the British leader, Winston Churchill, heard that he was standing down he wrote to him: " . . . you, more than any other man, have saved Western civilization."

Eleanor
ROOSEVELT (1884-1962)

F.D.R.'s formidable wife

★

Eleanor Roosevelt was the niece of President Theodore Roosevelt. In 1905, she married her distant cousin, Franklin, and when he embarked on his political career she campaigned long and hard for him. While taking an active interest in social work, youth movements and the rights of minority groups, she still found time to bring up six children!

Shortly after F.D.R. was elected to the White House, Eleanor became the first President's wife to give a press conference. She also wrote a regular newspaper column, called *My Day*, which was syndicated throughout America and read by millions.

In 1945, Eleanor was appointed a delegate to the United Nations, and from 1946-1951 she was chairman of the U.N. Human Rights Commission.

She wrote several books, hundreds of newspaper articles and, even toward the end of her life, she was embarking on lecture tours that would have exhausted women half her age.

★

Eleanor Roosevelt, the most versatile and accomplished first lady America has known. A tireless traveler, she circled the world several times, and met with many world leaders.

Gen. George S. ★★★★★★

PATTON (1885-1945) ★★★★★★

Larger-than-life soldier

★

George Smith Patton graduated from the U.S. Military Academy in 1909. In World War I he commanded an armored brigade in Europe.

During World War II, Patton led the first U.S. troops to fight in North Africa. Two years later he commanded the 7th Army in Sicily, and in 1944 he was back on the Western Front, in command of the 3rd Army. He led his men as they swept through France, and by the time they crossed the Rhine, the German army was virtually defeated.

A dedicated soldier himself, Patton demanded 100 per cent effort from his men, and once outraged his superiors by slapping a soldier he thought was malingering.

Patton disagreed with his political masters on how post-war Germany should be dealt with and was then transferred to the 5th Army, little more than a skeleton force. He was killed in an automobile accident while commanding the troops.

Patton, who died after an accident in Germany, was a colorful soldier, known as "Old Blood and Guts" to his troops. He was well-known, too, for his ruthless drive and disregard of classic military rules.

Al  JOLSON (1886-1950) ★★★★★★

The first man to talk in the movies

★

Young Asa Yoelson's parents wanted him to be a cantor at the local synagogue, but he had other ideas. He ran away from home and joined the circus.

He graduated to vaudeville and, with his famous trade mark of dressing as a minstrel and blacking his face, became the biggest star on Broadway.

In 1927, Warner Brothers cast Jolson in their first talkie, *The Jazz Singer*. The movie made him the first talking picture movie star.

When Jolson sang *Sonny Boy, Mammy* and the other sentimental songs he made famous, audiences wept. Critics said he didn't sing songs, he *sold* them to audiences.

Tastes change, and by 1944 Jolson's movie career was over. But when Columbia pictures decided to make *The Jolson Story*, they asked him to dub the songs for Larry Parks, who played the title role. The movie was a huge success and opened up a new career for Jolson as a radio and recording star. When he died, he left over $4 million.

★

Al Jolson, the great tearjerker.

Irving

BERLIN (b. 1888)

The man who wrote *God Bless America*

★

Irving Berlin came to America from Russia when he was five. Although he didn't have any formal music training, Berlin began to write songs. In 1911, while working as a singing waiter, he had his first hit with his song, *Alexander's Ragtime Band*.

Berlin's most famous songs were written for movies such as *Top Hat, Easter Parade, Annie Get Your Gun* and *Call Me Madam*.

The title song for the movie *White Christmas*, recorded by Bing Crosby in 1942, sold 30 million copies. It was the best-selling record of all time until Band Aid's *Do They Know It's Christmas?* broke the record more than 40 years later.

It's unusual that Berlin wrote more than 1,000 songs, yet never learned to read music. How did he do it? His songs were composed on a piano, which had been adapted to change key mechanically!

★

Irving Berlin – great composer.

Gen. Dwight D. ★★★★★

EISENHOWER (1890-1969) ★★★

Military leader and two-term President

★

Eisenhower – 34th President of the U.S.

Although Dwight "Ike" Eisenhower graduated top of his class from West Point in 1915 and was recognized as a brilliant organizer, he had only reached the rank of lieutenant-colonel when, in 1942, the United States entered World War II.

Eisenhower's military talents were outstanding. He was put in command of the Allied troops mustered for an attack on French North Africa. He so impressed his military and political masters with his ability to lead men, he was chosen as Supreme Commander of the Allied Expeditionary Force which invaded France in 1944. He had *3 million men* in his command.

On 6 June, the Allies crossed the English Channel and landed in Normandy. They swept through Europe, where Eisenhower made his one big mistake – he allowed the Russian Army to reach Berlin. After the war, Russia was the dominant influence in Eastern Europe.

Eisenhower was elected President in 1952 and re-elected in 1956, and his popularity as a war hero made him a national symbol.

President Eisenhower had time for fun too. Here he plays golf for the Heart Fund Gold Benefit Golf Match in 1964, shortly after his retirement.

Cole ★★★★★★★★★★

PORTER (1892-1964) ★★★★★★

The man whose songs made the world sing

★

The story of many songwriters is of rags to riches. Cole Porter's is one of rich to richer! He was born into a very wealthy Indiana family, who expected him to follow the family tradition and study law.

He went to Harvard University, but he spent more time writing songs for college revues than reading law books. In the face of strong family opposition, Porter quit law school and traveled to Paris to study music.

In 1928, Porter had his first Broadway success with a show called *Paris*. Thereafter, songs and shows gushed from him like oil from a rich well, and he became famous throughout the country.

Porter's shows, such as *Kiss Me Kate* and *Can Can*, were packed with memorable songs, notable for their clever, witty lyrics. His melodies were whistled by newsboys and played in stylish night clubs.

But for Porter, the climax of his career came toward the end of his life when the authorities of his old university conferred an honorary degree on him.

Cole Porter's most famous songs include Night and Day *and* Begin the Beguine.

Norman

★ ★ ★ ★ ★ ★ ★ ★ ★

ROCKWELL (1894-1978) ★ ★ ★ ★

America's best-known artist

★

As a schoolboy, Norman Rockwell was short-sighted and pigeon-toed and unable to play sports. So he turned to drawing, to amuse himself and his friends. It quickly became obvious he was extremely talented.

At 15, Rockwell was commissioned to draw four Christmas cards. At 17, he illustrated his first book, *Tell Me Why Stories*. At 19, he became art director on *Boy's Life*, the Boy Scout magazine.

When Rockwell was just 22, he drew his first cover for the famous *Saturday Evening Post*. It showed a disgusted boy pushing a baby carriage while his jeering friends went off to play baseball. The picture was a huge success. From then on, Rockwell drew an average of 10 *Post* covers a year.

Many art critics were scathing of Rockwell's work, but Americans loved the way his drawings captured ordinary folks doing ordinary things. Rockwell's paintings are portraits to be enjoyed not by visitors to the houses of wealthy art patrons, but by the millions of Americans who hang prints of his work on the walls of their homes.

★

Norman Rockwell, one of America's best-loved illustrators.

George "Babe" ★★★★★★★

RUTH (1895-1948) ★★★★★★★

The best baseball player ever

★

If you look through the baseball record books you may be surprised to read that one record has remained the same since 1921: 457 total bases in one American League season. The man who hit them was "Babe" Ruth, arguably the best baseball player of all time.

From an early age, Ruth was baseball mad, and when he was 19, he signed up as pitcher with the Boston Red Sox. Five years later, he moved to New York to play for the Yankees as an outfielder. He then returned to Boston in 1935, this time to play for the Bees.

Ruth hit a total 714 home runs in his career, a record 60 of them in the 1927 season. His three home runs in one game in 1926 was not equalled until 1977.

Ruth lived just as hard as he played. So much so, he was forced to miss the 1925 season because he was physically exhausted.

The Yankees obviously knew what an asset they had in Ruth, because in 1930-31 he was paid $80,000 – well over $1 million by today's standards.

"Babe" Ruth's record of 714 home runs was not beaten until 1974, by Hank Aaron.

F. Scott ★★★★★★★★★
FITZGERALD (1896-1940) ★★★

The prophet of the "Jazz Age"

★

F. Scott Fitzgerald, the great writer who died a broken man.

Francis Scott Fitzgerald began writing short stories as a schoolboy in St. Paul, Minnesota. In 1920, at the age of 24, his first full-length novel, *This Side of Paradise*, became an instant best-seller.

This was followed by several volumes of superb short stories and three unforgettable novels about the world F. Scott Fitzgerald knew – full of rich, frivolous, selfish characters, reflecting the "unreal" gloss of the 1920s. His book of short stories published in 1922 gave the decade its name – The Jazz Age.

Fitzgerald's finest novel, *The Great Gatsby*, published in 1925, brought him success and fame. As soon as he became successful he and his wife, Zelda, embarked on a life of traveling and party-going. Zelda suffered a severe nervous breakdown and was confined to a sanatorium.

Fitzgerald started drinking heavily and spent all the money he had made from his books on high-living. When he ran out of money he became a scriptwriter in Hollywood, where he died of a heart attack in 1940. He left an unfinished novel, *The Last Tycoon*, behind him, which was published after his death.

Amelia

EARHART (1898-1937)

First woman to fly solo across the Atlantic

★

In 1928, Amelia Earhart was asked to be a passenger on a flight from Newfoundland to Wales. She did, but was embarrassed by all the publicity she received as "the first woman to fly the Atlantic." After all, she hadn't *done* anything.

Therefore, she decided to *do* something. In May 1932, her airplane, a Lockheed Vega, took off from Newfoundland and landed the next day in Ireland.

Earhart became obsessed by flight. In 1935, she made the first flight from Hawaii to California.

In 1937, Earhart flew again, hoping to become the first to fly solo around the world above the equator. While she was flying somewhere between New Guinea and Howland Island in the Pacific, her airplane disappeared. No one knows what happened. Some believe that she crash-landed on a Japanese island, was taken prisoner and killed. More likely, her plane crashed into the sea and she was drowned somewhere in mid-ocean. Probably, we shall never know.

Amelia Earhart – heroic aviator.

Humphrey ★★★★★★★★

BOGART (1899-1957) ★★★★★★

The man who was "too ugly to play heroes"

★

When Humphrey Bogart was screen-tested, the movie men, noting his squint, the scar on his mouth, the odd, sneering smile and his slight lisp, decided he was so ugly he should play a gangster.

Bogart played gangsters in all his early movies, such as *The Petrified Forest* and *Angels with Dirty Faces*. But slowly, he changed his image and began to play "good guys," still tough and cynical, but men with a streak of kindness in them.

Bogart made 77 movies in all, including such classics as *The Maltese Falcon, Casablanca, The Big Sleep, The African Queen* and *The Caine Mutiny*.

He married Lauren Bacall, the teenage beauty who starred with him in *To Have and Have Not*.

Bogart died of cancer in 1957. He is still remembered as one of Hollywood's greatest stars and people still recall his famous line in *Casablanca* – "Play it again, Sam."

In fact, he never said it! All he actually said was: "Play it, Sam."

★

Humphrey Bogart as Philip Marlowe, the cool detective, in the film The Big Sleep.

Ernest ★★★★★★★★

HEMINGWAY (1899-1961) ★★★

Winner of the Pulitzer and Nobel prizes

★

Ernest Hemingway's father wanted him to follow in his footsteps and study medicine. But when he was 17, he left school and became a junior reporter on *The Kansas City Star*.

When World War I broke out, Hemingway was turned down for the army because he had bad eyesight. So he volunteered to be an ambulance driver and was sent to the Italian front.

After the war, Hemingway settled in Paris where he made friends with fellow American writers, Ezra Pound and Gertrude Stein, who had a great influence on him.

Hemingway traveled around Europe writing brilliant newspaper articles, and then returned to Paris to complete his first novel, *The Sun Also Rises*.

This was followed by *A Farewell to Arms*, inspired by his experiences in Italy as an ambulance driver. Thereafter, he divided his time between writing and fishing, going on safari and watching bullfights in Spain.

Ernest Hemingway – his energetic life ended in tragic suicide.

During the Spanish Civil War (1936-1939), Hemingway fought for the Republicans. His adventures provided the material for one of his greatest novels, *For Whom the Bell Tolls.*

Hemingway became a war correspondent during World War II, covering the Normandy landings and often flying on dangerous missions over Europe.

After the war, he won both the Pulitzer and the Nobel prize for literature for *The Old Man and the Sea.*

Hemingway could strip stories down to their basics without losing drama and power. Physically, he was tall and muscular. The combination of brain and brawn proved irresistible to readers.

When he was in Cuba, covering the Castro revolution, Hemingway realized that his eyesight was failing. He became so depressed as his health began to fail, he attempted suicide. He tried to shoot himself; he tried to jump out of an airplane; and he had to be physically restrained from walking into a moving airplane propeller.

Finally, in 1961, Hemingway put a shotgun to his head and pulled the trigger . . .

Hemingway with his wife, Mary, in the cabin of their 40-foot fishing boat the Pilar.

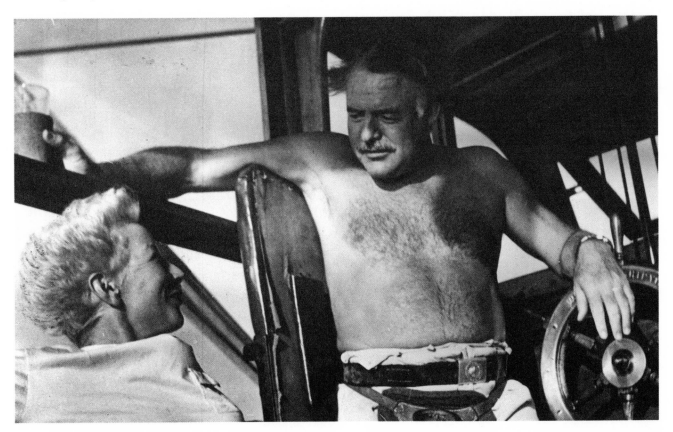

Walt ★★★★★★★★★★★★

DISNEY (1901-1966) ★★★★★★

The king of the cartoons

★

Walt Disney was born in Chicago, and after he left college he earned his living as a commercial artist.

In the mid-1920s, Disney hit upon the idea of making a cartoon movie, featuring a little mouse. The film was called *Steamboat Willie*, and Mickey Mouse made his debut on the silver screen.

By 1937, Disney had 700 people working on the first full-length cartoon, *Snow White and the Seven Dwarfs*. The critics said a musical cartoon would be a flop. But at the premiere, film moguls and their wives wept in their seats. Next came *Pinocchio, Bambi, Sleeping Beauty*, natural history movies, and, finally, full-length features.

Walt Disney's world lives on in Disneyland, California, and Disney World, Florida.

Disney didn't draw his famous cartoon characters himself. In fact, he couldn't even sign his name the same way twice! It was someone else who wrote the famous Walt Disney signature that appears on every Disney film. But Disney had all the ideas, and he was a brilliant businessman.

Disney did, however, feature in the early *Mickey Mouse* movies. It was he who supplied Mickey Mouse's voice in the first cartoons.

Clark ★★★★★★★★★

GABLE (1901-1960) ★★★★★★

Hollywood heart-throb

★

When telephone repair man Clark Gable went to fix a client's phone, he had no idea that she was a drama coach. She took a liking to the handsome young man, gave him acting lessons and got him into the movies.

Gable played supporting roles to Joan Crawford and other stars, but when a movie called *It Happened One Night* was released, Gable became a star himself. In the movie, Gable took off his shirt, and audiences all over America were shocked to see he wasn't wearing an undershirt. Overnight, undershirt sales slumped!

Gable went on to star in some of Hollywood's most famous films, such as *Mutiny on the Bounty* and *San Francisco.* When MGM were casting *Gone With the Wind* there was only one candidate for the male lead – Clark Gable. The film made Gable the Hollywood heart-throb of all time.

Nothing Gable did after that matched the success of *Gone With the Wind.* Gable died just before his last movie, *The Misfits,* was released.

★

Clark Gable, the king of Hollywood.

Charles ★★★★★★★★★

LINDBERGH (1902-1974) ★★★★

The first man to fly solo across the Atlantic

★

In 1919, a prize of $25,000 was offered to whoever made the first solo flight from New York to Paris. Six men died in the attempt before Charles Lindbergh made it in 1927.

Lindbergh had little money of his own, but he was so enthusiastic that his fellow citizens of St. Louis held a collection for him.

On May 20, 1927, Lindbergh took off from New York in the 220-horsepower airplane, *The Spirit of St. Louis*, and narrowly missed crashing into the wires at the end of the runway.

Lindbergh, the "Spirit of St. Louis."

During the flight the airplane's wings iced over. Then the plane almost crashed into the ocean when it went into an involuntary spin. Lindbergh almost fell asleep several times, but 33½ hours after take-off, he landed just outside Paris. America had a new hero.

Lindbergh hit the headlines again five years later, when his baby son was kidnapped. Although he paid a ransom of $50,000, the infant was eventually found dead.

In 1954, Lindbergh won the Pulitzer Prize for his autobiography called, appropriately, *The Spirit of St. Louis*.

Richard

★★★★★★★★★

RODGERS (1902-1979) ★★★★★

Composer of Broadway's most popular shows

★

Richard Rodgers began piano lessons when he was six and wrote his first song, *Camptown Days*, when he was only 12. In 1918, he met a young lyricist, Lorenz Hart, and two years later the pair wrote a revue for Columbia University. It was the first of many shows they wrote together. They had their first Broadway success in 1925 with *Garrick Gaieties*, and their last, 15 years later, with *Pal Joey*.

Richard Rodgers, great American composer.

After Hart's death in 1943, Rodgers worked with Oscar Hammerstein. They won two Pulitzer Prizes – for *Oklahoma* in 1943, and *South Pacific* in 1949. Ten years later Broadway was enraptured by *The Sound of Music*, which later became one of Hollywood's most successful movies.

Rodgers was one of Broadway's most productive and important composers. His shows were musical plays rather than musical comedies, which had entertained theater audiences for decades. When he died, the lights were dimmed on Broadway, a tribute which is reserved only for our greatest showmen.

Johnny ★★★★★★★★★
WEISSMULLER (1904-1984) ★★

Hollywood's favorite Tarzan

★

At the 1924 Paris Olympics, Johnny Weissmuller broke three swimming records. After the 1928 Amsterdam games, he became a professional athlete.

When Weissmuller was on vacation in California, MGM asked him to test for the part of Tarzan, the English lord lost in a plane crash and reared by apes in the Amazon jungle. The movie, *Tarzan the Ape Man*, was a smash hit. Weissmuller swung through the trees like an ape, swam like a fish and wrestled with alligators.

This was followed by a hugely successful series of *Tarzan* movies. Each one took about three weeks to shoot, and Weissmuller was paid at least $100,000 a movie.

Weissmuller retired to Florida in 1958, but was tempted back to Hollywood to make two more movies – *The Phynx* and *The Dog Who Saved Hollywood*. Out of the jungle, Weissmuller was out of his depth and the movies bombed. That did not alter the fact, however, that, to the movie-goers of the 1930s and 1940s, Johnny Weissmuller *was* Tarzan.

Weissmuller as Tarzan in the film Tarzan the Ape Man, *1932.*

Prof. Indiana

★★★★★★★

JONES (b. circa 1906) ★★★★★★

The man who found the lost ark

★

Indiana Jones is the creation of one of America's most successful film directors/producers, Steven Spielberg. He has featured in two major films, *Raiders of the Lost Ark* and *Return to the Temple of Doom*.

In 1936, Prof. Indiana Jones, usually a quiet, academic man with an interest in rare treasures, was approached by the curator of the National Museum in Washington. He told Jones the Nazis were on the trail of the Ark of the Covenant – the chest in which the Jews had put the stones bearing the Ten Commandments.

Jones set off to ensure the treasure did not fall into Nazi hands, and to bring the ark back to America.

He returned to academic life, but it was not too long before he was off on his travels again, this time pitting his wits against the evil guardians of the Temple of Doom.

Jones bears an uncanny resemblance to East Coast cop Joe Book, space cavalier Han Solo, android-fighter Rick Deckard and Hollywood movie star Harrison Ford (who played them all).

★

Indiana Jones, played by actor Harrison Ford, in Return to the Temple of Doom.

John  WAYNE (1907-1979)

Superstar of the Hollywood Western

★

When Marion Morrison was a child, his parents moved to a homestead in California, where he became an excellent horseback rider. After high school, Marion decided to break into the movies, and went to Hollywood. He changed his name to John Wayne, and got a job as a prop boy on one of the studio backlots.

Wayne began to get bit-parts in movies, and then graduated to speaking roles. In 1939, director John Ford chose him to play the starring role in *Stagecoach*. As soon as the film was released, John Wayne was an instant star.

Wayne stayed at the top of his profession until his death in 1979, making more than 80 films, most of them Westerns. He earned more than $400 million . . . and lost most of it in bad investments.

In 1969, Wayne won the Oscar for his part as a washed-out marshal in *True Grit*, and a few years later he played a gunfighter dying of cancer in *The Shootist*. This was his last film because, sadly, Wayne was, himself, dying of cancer.

★

John Wayne, Hollywood's greatest cowboy.

Errol ★★★★★★★★★★ FLYNN (1909-1959) ★★★★★★

Swashbuckling screen hero

★

Errol Flynn's early life was as adventurous as some of the heroes he later played. Before he became an actor, Flynn prospected for gold, smuggled diamonds and stood trial for murder in New Guinea, Africa.

He decided he wanted to be an actor. He traveled to England and worked in summer stock before making a movie – *Murder in Monte Carlo*. A talent scout from Warner Brothers saw it and offered Flynn a contract at $150 a week.

Flynn played small parts before he was cast as the swashbuckling Captain Blood. This was followed by a variety of movies, including *The Adventures of Robin Hood, The Sea Hawk* and *They Died with Their Boots On*, in which he played General Custer.

Toward the end of his career, Flynn played drunks in two movies. He was well cast, for by this time he was drinking heavily. When he died of a heart attack, the coroner said that he had the body of an old, tired man – a sad end for one of Hollywood's most dashing stars.

★

Errol Flynn – wine, women and fisticuffs!

Tennessee ★★★★★★★★

WILLIAMS (1911-1983) ★★★★★

Pulitzer Prize-winning playwright

★

During the Great Depression of 1929, Tennessee Williams, born Thomas Lanier Williams, worked in a factory and waited on tables in his home town, St. Louis, Missouri. When he graduated from university he started to write plays.

In 1939, Williams was awarded a Theater Guild prize for four one-act plays. His first full-length work was a flop, but his second, *The Glass Menagerie*, was a great success.

Shortly after he began work on *A Streetcar Named Desire* in 1946, he became ill. Thinking he was going to die, he worked day and night to finish the play. He recovered – and the play won the Pulitzer Prize. (It also gave Marlon Brando his big break on Broadway, playing the anti-hero, Stanley Kowalski.) Williams won the Pulitzer Prize again in 1955 for *Cat on a Hot Tin Roof*.

Most of Tennessee Williams's plays are set in the deep South. They are controversial, often dealing with unpleasant characters, but Williams was, without doubt, one of America's greatest playwrights.

Tennessee Williams, playwright of the South.

Roy ★★★★★★★★★★★★
ROGERS (b. 1912) ★★★★★★

Hero of B-feature cowboy movies

★

If you went to the movies in the 1940s and 1950s, you'd almost certainly see a B-movie as well as the main feature.

B-movies were usually shot in black and white, made on a small budget and, more often than not, they were Westerns.

Roy Rogers was the king of the B-movies. He rode onto the screen in countless movies with his horse, Trigger, strumming his guitar and singing a folksy song about his "one-two-three-four-legged, four-legged friend."

Rogers was probably the most wholesome hero of all time. He never killed wrong-doers, but always managed to bring them to justice. Trigger the horse, a magnificent palomino, could untie ropes, gallop riderless across the prairie to summon help when Roy was in danger, disarm gun-slingers and even cover himself with blankets when it was time to sleep!

Critics thought Trigger was a better actor than Rogers, but there is no denying that Rogers, his wife, Dale, and Trigger brought immense pleasure to countless American moviegoers.

Roy Rogers and his faithful horse, Trigger.

Jackson
★★★★★★★★
POLLOCK (1912-1956)
★★★★★

America's foremost modern artist

★

Jackson Pollock – abstract expressionist.

Like many young artists of the early 20th century, Jackson Pollock was influenced by Picasso and other "modern artists." But he went on to establish a style of his own, which is now called "abstract expressionism."

Pollock abandoned paint brushes, preferring to drip aluminum paint and enamels onto huge canvases, building up patterns of fine lines and huge splodges of color. He used pebbles, shells, bits of string and glass – anything he felt would give his paintings texture. He usually worked with his enormous canvases on the floor.

Pollock's first one-man show in 1943 in New York City was a sensation. By 1948 he was recognized as America's leading artist but, despite his success, he was a heavy drinker and smoker, and under constant psychiatric care.

Sadly, Pollock was killed in an automobile accident on Long Island. Seventeen years after his death, one of his paintings, *Blue Poles*, was sold for $2 million – the highest price ever paid for an American painting at the time.

Jesse

OWENS (1913-1980)

The black athlete who made Hitler furious

★

The 1936 Olympic games were to be a showplace for Adolph Hitler's Germany. He hoped that white athletes would win all the medals and prove his theory that whites, or Arians, were superior to every other race.

Jesse Owens put paid to that.

Owens came from a poor family, and as a child all he wanted to do was run and run. By the time he was 20, he was America's fastest sprinter. One afternoon in 1935, he equalled one world record and broke five more.

At the Olympics, with Hitler in the crowd, Owens won gold medals in the 100m, 200m and the 400m relay. In the long jump, he won the gold with a leap of 26′ 5½″, after almost failing to qualify in the first round.

Hitler was so furious with Owens, he refused to shake hands with him. But when Owens returned to New York, he was given a ticker-tape welcome – a fitting tribute to the man who beat Hitler at his own games.

★

Owens goes for gold at the 1936 Olympics.

Joe ★★★★★★★★★★
DiMAGGIO (b. 1914) ★★★★★

Baseball's "Yankee Clipper"

★

When Joe DiMaggio was at school his father was too poor to buy him baseball gear. That didn't stop DiMaggio becoming the best player in school.

DiMaggio was signed for the San Francisco Seals in 1932. Two years later, he was acknowledged the greatest player the Coast League had ever produced. In 1935 it cost the New York Yankees $75,000 to sign him.

Di Maggio was voted *Sporting News'* most valuable player in the league in 1939. He was one of the few league players to hit two home runs in a single inning and, without doubt, the best-known baseball player of his day.

When DiMaggio married in 1954, his wedding seemed like a fairytale: DiMaggio, the son of a poor crab fisherman, was the most famous sportsman in America; his bride was the best-known movie star in the world – Marilyn Monroe. But the marriage lasted only nine months, and, as his career came to an end, DiMaggio, rather than being famous as a great sportsman, was better known as one of Marilyn Monroe's ex-husbands.

Joe DiMaggio.

Joe DiMaggio with a young fan.

Joe ★★★★★★★★★★
LOUIS (1914-1981) ★★★★★★★

"The Brown Bomber"

★

Joe Louis's parents wanted him to be a violinist, but Joe spent the money he was given for lessons on boxing training sessions instead.

He trained hard and won the amateur heavyweight title before turning professional in 1934. The next year, he beat former world champ Primo Carnera in the seventh round, but a year later was beaten by the German Max Schmeling.

In 1937, Louis took the world heavyweight title when he knocked out Jimmy Braddock, and in 1938 he had his revenge on Schmeling by knocking him out in the first round!

Louis retired in 1949, undefeated after 25 title fights. He was tempted back into the ring a year later but, sadly, he was outpointed by Ezzard Charles and lost his bid to regain the world heavyweight title.

In all of Louis's professional career, only three boxers ever beat him – Schmeling, Charles and, in 1951, Rocky Marciano, who knocked him out.

Joe Louis' real name was Joseph Louis Barrow. But everyone knew him as the "Brown Bomber."

"Red"

ADAIR (b. 1915)

Trouble-shooting oil man

★

One of the greatest fears that oil men have is that their wells will catch fire. If this happens, with millions of gallons of crude oil underground, the fire can burn for months before it dies out.

That's where "Red" Adair comes in. His full name is Paul Neal Adair, and his official title is oil well control specialist. He seems to know instinctively how a fire will run its course and how best to douse the flames.

From 1939 until the mid-1950s, Adair worked for a company that specialized in controlling oil fires. He established a reputation as a fearless expert who had put his life at risk many times in the course of his job.

In 1959, he founded the Red Adair Fire and Blowout Control Co. Since then he has been hired by oil companies from Texas to the North Sea in Europe whenever disaster has struck. His fees are said to be high, but his courage and skill have saved the oil moguls hundreds of millions of dollars.

★

Oil disaster expert Red Adair looks confident on his way to a blowout at an oilfield.

John F.

KENNEDY (1917-1963) ★★★★★

The youngest occupant of the Oval Office

★

"Jack" Fitzgerald Kennedy was born in Boston, where both his grandmother and father had been prominent politicians. His parents were immensely rich, and devout Roman Catholics.

Part of Kennedy's childhood was spent in London, England, where his father was U.S. Ambassador. In 1936, he went to Harvard University, and damaged his spine in a football game. The injury caused him pain for the rest of his life, but it didn't stop him joining the Navy when the United States entered World War II.

When Kennedy's boat was sunk by a Japanese destroyer, he saved the lives of several of his crew. He was awarded the Purple Heart and the Navy and Marine Corps Medals for his bravery.

Kennedy's father always intended that John's brother, Joe, would lead the next generation of Kennedy politicians. But when Joe was killed in the war, the family's political ambitions turned to the young John.

★

J.F. Kennedy – 35th President of the U.S.

Kennedy was elected to the Massachusetts House of Representatives in 1946 and to the U.S. Senate in 1952, where he gained a wealth of political experience. In 1960, he was selected on the first ballot at the National Democratic Party convention to run for President. He scraped home by just 120,000 popular votes.

Kennedy put more than 1,000 bills before Congress, many aimed at improving the U.S. economy. In 1962, 200,000 civil rights supporters marched on Washington D.C. in support of his Civil Rights Bill.

In 1962, Kennedy demanded Russian missile bases in Cuba be dismantled. For several days, the world hovered on the brink of war before Russia backed down. Thereafter, relations between America and Russia thawed.

John F. Kennedy (far left) with his brothers Robert and Edward. Robert, also a prominent politician, was tragically shot dead in 1968.

In November 1963, Kennedy was visiting Dallas, Texas. As his motorcade passed the Texas School Book Depository, a man named Lee Harvey Oswald shot him. Kennedy slumped forward next to his wife, Jackie. He died shortly afterward.

Such was the impact of Kennedy's death, even now, over 20 years later, hundreds of millions of people around the world can remember exactly where they were and what they were doing when they heard John F. Kennedy had been shot.

Leonard

BERNSTEIN (b. 1918)

America's leading man of music

★

In 1943, when Bruno Walter was unable to conduct the New York Philharmonic for an important concert, Leonard Bernstein, a young unknown, who had graduated from music college just two years before, was asked to stand in. He was an overnight sensation.

Two years later, Bernstein became director of the New York City Symphony. He began to appear all over the world as guest conductor with major orchestras, and wrote his first symphony in 1942.

A scene from West Side Story. *Here Bernardo, of the Sharks, challenges Riff of the rival gang, the Jets.*

Leonard Bernstein conducts the New York City Symphony.

In 1958, Bernstein's *West Side Story*, a modern-day *Romeo and Juliet*, opened on Broadway and ran for 734 performances. When it was filmed, it won the Oscar for the best movie of 1961.

Bernstein is one of America's most versatile composers. When the Kennedy Center for Performing Arts was opened in 1971, it was Bernstein's especially-commissioned *Mass* that was chosen for the opening concert.

Judy

GARLAND (1922-1969) ★★★★★

The over-the-rainbow girl

★

At the age of three, Frances Gumm was already singing on stage with her two elder sisters. In 1935, when she was just 13, she was given a contract by MGM, who changed her name to Judy Garland, and cast her in a handful of low-budget movies.

When MGM was casting *The Wizard of Oz*, they were desperate to get Shirley Temple to play Dorothy, the lead part, but her studio wouldn't release her from her contract. So, MGM cast Judy Garland in the part . . . and she became the studio's biggest star.

Judy Garland as Dorothy, in The Wizard of Oz.

Garland went on to make some of the best Hollywood musicals, and soon showed that she could act just as well as she could sing. But then, she became addicted to pills and drink. She became so difficult to work with, the studio eventually canceled her contract.

Garland toured America and Europe. Wherever she sang, audiences flocked to hear her sing *Over the Rainbow, The Man that Got Away,* and other favorites. But sadly, the pills and the alcohol took their toll. Garland's performances suffered, and she died of an accidental drug overdose in London.

Rocky ★★★★★★★★★

MARCIANO (1923-1969) ★★★★

"The Rock with the sock"

★

Rocco Marchegiano started to box when he was a serviceman in Britain during World War II. By 1947, he had built up such a reputation as an amateur heavyweight that he turned pro and changed his name to Rocky Marciano.

Marciano didn't have much style, but he had a knock-out punch in both fists. In his first 42 fights he wasn't even knocked off his feet, and finished all but five of them before the match could finish.

Rocky Marciano, with the "knock-out" punch.

His 43rd fight, in 1952, was against Jersey Joe Woolcott – the world champion. Jersey Joe had Marciano on the floor for a count of three in the early stages of the fight, but in the 13th round Marciano landed an amazing right-hand punch on his opponent and the fight was over.

By the time he announced his retirement in 1956, Marciano had defended his title six times, he had knocked out three world champions (Joe Louis, Joe Walcott and Ezzard Charles) and hadn't lost a single fight as a professional.

Sadly, Marciano was killed in an air crash.

Audie ★★★★★★★★★★
MURPHY (1924-1971) ★★★★★

The war hero who became an actor

★

Audie Murphy worked as a sharecropper, garage attendant and a clerk when he came out of the army after World War II. Then, in 1948, he was cast in his first movie, *Beyond Glory*. It wasn't a great success, but director John Huston saw it and cast Murphy as a young soldier in *The Red Badge of Courage*, a box office hit.

Murphy was not the greatest screen actor. After he'd made a string of Westerns he said, "The script's always the same, only the horses change."

Toward the end of his life, Murphy was actively engaged in fighting drug-runners. He died in a plane crash in Virginia.

Murphy's best-known movie was *To Hell and Back*, in which he played America's most decorated war hero – the man who won the Congressional Medal of Honor, Distinguished Service Cross, Silver Star, Legion of Merit, Bronze Star and Purple Heart with two oak leaf clusters. What was the name of this hero? Major Audie Murphy!

★

Murphy, the most decorated war hero of the U.S.

Johnny ★★★★★★★★★★
CARSON (b. 1925) ★★★★★★

America's chat show king

★

Johnny Carson was born in Iowa, and became famous when he hosted a quiz show called *Earn Your Vacation*. He became so well-known that when, in 1962, NBC were looking for someone to replace the argumentative Jack Paar on the *Tonight Show* they asked Carson to take over.

Previous presenters had played second fiddle to the stars and personalities they introduced and interviewed. Carson became *the* star of the show. As soon as Ed McMahon announces "Heeeeeeere's Johnny!" there's no doubt that it's the Johnny Carson show.

Johnny – "Heeeeeeere's Johnny" – Carson.

Over the years, every top U.S. star and visiting personality from Europe has appeared on the show. As well as hosting the *Tonight Show*, which goes out for one hour, four times a week, Carson has hosted the Oscar awards and other gala events.

Carson is the highest-paid performer on television. He earns $5 million a year from the show, which has made him an incredibly rich man. When he and his wife divorced in 1984, she was awarded more than $20 million in alimony.

Marilyn ★★★★★★★★★

MONROE (1926-1962) ★★★★★

The "dumb blonde" who could act like a goddess

★

Norma Jean Mortenson spent most of her childhood in orphanages, day-dreaming of becoming a movie star.

By the time Norma Jean was 21, she had divorced her first husband and was earning a living modeling for calendars. In the early 1950s, she changed her name to Marilyn Monroe and tested for a tiny screen role as a "dumb blonde." She was on the screen for no more than a minute or two, but that was enough for everyone to see that she had true film-star quality.

Monroe played many small roles before people realized that she was a brilliant comedienne. She won wide acclaim for her role in *Some Like It Hot*.

Like many stars of the time, Monroe was highly-strung and almost impossible to work with. In 1961, she appeared in *The Misfits*, a serious drama. Shortly afterward, she was found dead in her bed, apparently from a drug overdose.

There has never been another star like the "blonde bombshell," Marilyn Monroe.

★

Marylin Monroe was, at one time, married to baseball star Joe DiMaggio.

Shirley

TEMPLE (b. 1928)

Hollywood's most famous child star

★

Little Shirley Temple could barely talk when her mother took her around the Hollywood studios, hoping to get her into the movies. When Mrs. Temple heard that Twentieth Century Fox were looking for a little girl to sing in one of their movies, Shirley auditioned and got the part.

The world fell in love with the cute little girl with the cute little voice, and when she sang *On the Good Ship Lollipop* in the movie, *Bright Eyes*, Temple became an instant star. By 1936, she was the world's top box-office draw. She could dance and sing, and when she cried the audiences reached for their tissues.

Although Temple never made the transition from child star to mature actress, she took it with good grace. "As an actress," she said, "I class myself with Rin Tin Tin."

When Temple retired from full-time movie making she had made 52 movies and had been the biggest star in Hollywood. She was 22! She went on to become a U.S. ambassador.

★

Shirley Temple was the No 1 American box office attraction from 1935-1938. People said her films were always fun because she was always the most sensible person in them!

Martin Luther KING (1929-1968)

The grandson of a slave and inspiring civil rights leader

★

Martin Luther King was born on January 15, 1929. His father was a well-to-do preacher.

King had a happy childhood in a large house in Atlanta and often played with white youngsters. When they were all old enough to go to school, he had to go to one for black children.

Shortly afterward, King asked his friends' mother why he was no longer allowed to play with them. "They're getting too old to play with niggers!" she said.

Martin Luther King – man of the people.

King ran home in tears. His mother tried to soothe him. "You're as good as anyone else," she said, "and don't forget it."

He never forgot. King fought racial prejudice until he died.

In 1954, after he had graduated from Boston University, King moved to Montgomery, Alabama, where he quickly became a leading spokesman for all the blacks in the city, throughout the state and, later, the whole country.

King made speech after speech, advocating racial equality. But he refused to have anything to do with violence. He was determined that the demonstrations he organized to demand civil rights for all blacks should be peaceful.

He was arrested. His home was bombed. But nothing deterred him.

In 1963, King addressed a rally of 250,000 people in Washington. "I have a dream . . ." he said, " . . . all God's children will join hands to sing 'Free at Last!'"

The next year, Martin Luther King won the Nobel peace prize.

In 1968, King was visiting Memphis, Tennessee. He was standing on the balcony of his hotel room with some colleagues when a shot rang out . . .

. . . a bullet hit him on the right side of his neck. He died in hospital an hour later.

Mainly due to his tireless campaigning, by the time King died he had seen the Civil Rights Bill become law in 1964, and the following year the Voting Rights Bill passed.

Blacks still faced, and face, racial prejudice in some parts of America, but thanks to the work of Martin Luther King, blacks and whites are equal in the eyes of American law.

Martin Luther King escorts black schoolchildren in Grenada, Mississippi, on their first day at a formerly all-white school, 1966.

Neil

ARMSTRONG (b. 1930) ★★★

The first man to walk on the Moon

★

Neil Armstrong who, with his colleague, Edwin Aldrin, landed on the Moon, southwest of the Sea of Tranquility.

Neil Armstrong was fresh out of high school when he joined the U.S. Navy to train as a fighter pilot. He flew 78 combat missions in the Korean War, where he gained a reputation for his coolness in the face of danger.

In 1955, Armstrong became a civilian test pilot for NASA and during his time there he flew higher and faster than any man had before – up to 20,000 feet at over 4,000 miles per hour.

When NASA began to train potential astronauts, Armstrong was included. In 1966, he was at the controls of *Gemini 8* when it went into a dangerous spin. Remaining quite calm, he made a successful emergency landing.

Armstrong was selected as command pilot for *Apollo II*, which was scheduled to make the first Moon landing. On July 20, 1969, with the world watching their television screens, Neil Armstrong clambered down the ladder of the space capsule and took his historic walk on the moon. He described this momentous occasion as, ". . . one small step for a man; one giant leap for Mankind."

Clint  ★★★★★★★★★★

EASTWOOD (b. 1930) ★★★★★

Screen tough-guy

★

Clint Eastwood is remembered by his school friends as the best basketball player in high school. He is remembered by rookies in the army as a great swimming instructor. He will be remembered by millions of movie fans as the nameless hero of *A Fistful of Dollars* and other "spaghetti Westerns."

Before he became famous, Eastwood appeared in small roles in dozens of movies and then hit the big time in the TV series, *Rawhide*.

After the "spaghetti Westerns," so called because they were made by Italian film makers, Eastwood played tough-guy cops in films such as *Dirty Harry, Magnum Force* and *The Enforcer*, and co-starred with a monkey in the comedies *Every Which Way But Loose* and *Any Which Way You Can*.

In 1986, Eastwood was voted mayor of Carmel, the picturesque Californian town where he lives, but denied that he would use this as a stepping stone for higher political office, like fellow movie star Ronald Reagan.

★

Clint Eastwood as The Outlaw Josey Wales.

Andy
WARHOL (1931-1987)

The originator of Pop Art

★

After graduating from the Carnegie Institute of Technology, Warhol, a tall, gawky man with a shock of straight fair hair, worked as a shoe designer. He was fascinated by everyday objects such as soup cans, and in 1962 his painting of 200 cans of Campbell's soup shocked the world.

Most critics thought the Campbell's painting was pointless, but others hailed it as a masterpiece. His pictures of movie stars, such as Elizabeth Taylor and Marilyn Monroe, were just as odd, but many people of Warhol's generation loved them.

Warhol surrounded himself with eccentric actors and artists in his New York "factory," where they made films that were even odder than his paintings. One, simply called *Sleep*, was three hours long and featured nothing but a sleeping man!

Warhol died in the hospital in 1987. His works now hang in galleries all over the world. Warhol is regarded by the art world as one of the most influential artists of this century.

Andy Warhol – Pop Art king.

James DEAN (1931-1955) ★★★★★★★

Star . . . of just three movies

★

In the 1950s, many teenagers were angry and rebellious. James Dean was both of these – and he was also an extremely gifted actor.

In 1955, Dean was chosen to play a young man who was jealous of the favoritism shown to his brother by their father. The film was *East of Eden*, and his performance captured the restlessness of his generation.

Dean's next movie was *Rebel Without a Cause*, in which he played a teenager who was desperate to prove himself to his family and friends. After the film was released, Dean became the hottest property in Hollywood.

James Dean, the youthful Hollywood legend.

For his third starring role, Dean chose the lead in *Giant*. He had to appear as a corrupt old man in the last reel, and everyone who worked on the movie with him agreed that it was a breathtaking performance.

Just before the movie was released, Dean bought a powerful new sports car. The English actor Sir Ralph Richardson pleaded with him not to drive it, but Dean roared off . . . he was killed in an automobile accident a few hours later.

Dean's death changed him from a cult hero into a Hollywood legend.

Woody
ALLEN (b. 1935)

Oscar-winning writer and director

★

Even when he was a schoolboy, Woody Allen was writing funny stories and selling them to New York newspapers. After graduation he worked as a scriptwriter for several leading TV comedians.

In 1965, Allen was asked to write the script and appear in a movie called *What's New Pussycat?*, which he later disowned!

Four years later, Allen got his first real break when he wrote *Take the Money and Run*, which he starred in and directed. Since then, he has written, directed and appeared in some of the best movies of the 1970s and 80s, including *Annie Hall, Manhattan, Broadway Danny Rose, Zelig* and *Hannah and Her Sisters*.

Most of Allen's films are set in New York City, where he was born and raised. Although he has won several Oscars for his films, he never goes to Hollywood to collect them. The Oscar ceremony is held on a Monday evening, and every Monday evening Allen plays his clarinet in a jazz bar in Manhattan!

★

Woody Allen is America's best-loved neurotic. He hates the countryside, alcohol, marriage, meeting people, vacations, and everything to do with films except writing the scripts!

Elvis ★★★★★★★★★★★

PRESLEY (1935-1977) ★★★★★

"The King"

★

In 1953, a record producer heard a "demo" disc that Elvis Presley had made as a present for his mother. The producer coaxed Presley into the studios to record *That's All Right.*

By 1955, three of his records had hit the Memphis charts and when Presley appeared in Jacksonville, Florida, police had to be called in to control the screaming teenagers.

A year later, millions heard him sing *Heartbreak Hotel* on television. Within a few days it was number one in the charts. "The King" – the most successful rock 'n roll singer of all time – had arrived.

Elvis Presley gyrates in Jailhouse Rock.

By the end of his career Presley had sold 155 million singles and 40 million albums and extended players. He also appeared in several hit movies.

During the 1960s, Presley's public appearances became rarer and rarer. When he re-emerged with a successful nightclub act, he was flabby and unfit. His health began to suffer.

When Presley died in 1977, television programs were interrupted with the news: "The King is dead."

Buddy
HOLLY (1936-1959)

The squeaky-clean pop star

★

In an era when other pop stars were noted for their rebellious behavior, Buddy Holly, with his shy smile and horn-rimmed glasses, looked and behaved like the boy next door.

Holly was born in Lubbock, Texas, and when he was still at high school he had his own show on a local radio station. By the time he was 19 he had his own group, the Crickets. The group became so well known locally that when Bill Haley and the Comets appeared in Lubbock, they asked the boys to appear with them.

That was the group's big break. A talent scout in the audience was so impressed that he arranged for them to make a "demo" disc.

But Buddy Holly and the Crickets had to wait until *That'll Be the Day* was released, two years later, for their first hit. It was followed by some of the best records of the 1950s.

In 1959, Holly was killed in a plane crash. Although his career lasted only two years, it was filled with more rock 'n roll classics than most pop stars achieve in careers lasting 10 times as long.

Buddy Holly sings "Peggy Sue," one of his greatest hits.

SUPERMAN (b. 1938) ★★★★★

Savior of civilization – several times over

★

What the elderly Kent couple didn't know when they found an abandoned baby was that it came from the distant planet Krypton. They called him Clark.

As he grew up, Kent developed superhuman strength. Even as a toddler he was strong enough to lift his foster-father's truck to help the old man change a wheel.

Kent got a job in the city of Metropolis as a junior reporter on *The Daily Planet.* On his first day, he was sent on an assignment with fellow reporter, Lois Lane. When they reached the company heliport there was an accident that left Lois dangling from the helicopter tail, more than a thousand feet above the sidewalk.

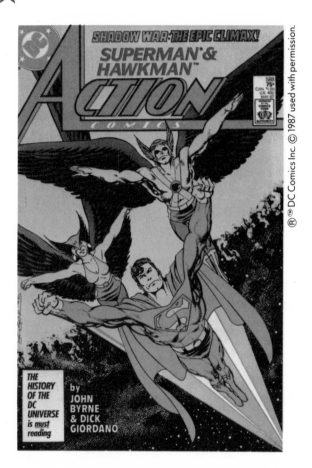

Superman flies to the rescue on the cover of DC Action Comic.

Quick as a flash, Kent disappeared into a handy phone booth and emerged, a split second later, in blue tights and red pants as Superman.

He could fly; he had X-ray vision; and whenever danger threatened, Superman came to the rescue.

The all-American comic strip superhero was first created by Jerry Siegel and Joe Shuster, both 17 years old at the time.

Dick RUTAN (b. 1938) ★★★★★

Jeanna YEAGER (b. 1952) ★★★

Flew non-stop around the world without refueling

★

Dick Rutan's brother, Burt, always wanted to build a plane that could fly around the world without stopping to refuel. One night in 1981, he sketched out the layout of *Voyager* on the back of a paper napkin.

Six years later, on December 14, 1986, Dick Rutan and his co-pilot, Jeanna Yeager, took off from Edwards Air Force Base in *Voyager*. Eighty per cent of the weight of the plane was accounted for by 1,200 gallons of fuel. As they were taxiing along the runway they damaged the wing-tip sails and had to jettison them, making the flight even more hazardous.

The two became so tired they had to use oxygen to keep awake. Yeager became violently ill when she took over the controls, and 20,000 feet over Africa she lost consciousness. Rutan was constantly worried that the fuel would run out.

But 216 hours and 25,012 miles after Rutan and Yeager set off, they landed back at Edwards Air Base where a crowd of 50,000 were waiting to welcome the two heroes who circumnavigated the earth without refueling.

Rutan and Yeager, shortly before take-off in Voyager.

★

Barbra  STREISAND (b. 1942)

Singing and screen superstar

★

When she was 18, Barbra Streisand won a singing competition in a New York City nightclub. She performed in several clubs until she got her first Broadway role in *I Can Get It From You Wholesale*, for which she won the first of her many awards.

The film *Funny Girl* brought her an Oscar. She won Emmies for her first album, *The Barbra Streisand Album*, and her first television special, *My Name Is Barbra*.

Streisand's performance in *What's Up Doc?* showed that she was one of the funniest actresses in Hollywood. The way she produced, directed, co-wrote, starred and sang in *Yentel* proved she was also a formidable business woman. She now has total control of every movie and album she makes.

Streisand has been called a "tiger" – an appropriate description for a woman whose fingernails (which she started to grow when she was waiting tables in a Chinese restaurant) are among the longest in Hollywood!

★

Barbra Streisand – outstanding performer.

Muhammad  ALI (b. 1942)

The greatest boxer of all time?

★

Cassius Marcellus Clay was born into a poor black family in Louisville, Kentucky. At the age of 12, he won his first amateur fight, and six years later he won the heavyweight boxing gold medal at the Rome Olympics.

Shortly afterward, he turned professional and won 19 fights in a row before he was given a chance to fight for the world championship in 1964.

His opponent was Sonny Liston, an enormous man who shuffled around the ring waiting for his chance to land his fearful knockout punch. Clay, by contrast, was light on his feet, skipping around the ring, constantly punching his opponents with the fastest left jab ever seen in a heavyweight.

Before the fight, Clay said he would "float like a butterfly and sting like a bee." The fight was over in seven rounds. Clay was world champion.

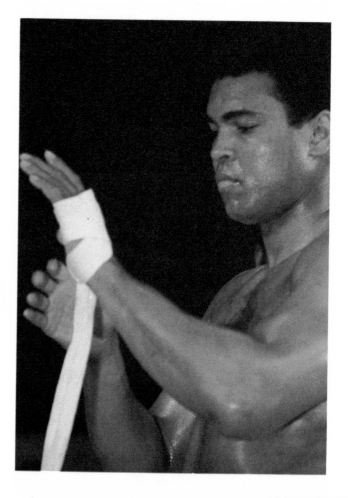

Muhammad Ali prepares for a big fight in Munich, 1976.

116

Cassius Clay, as he was then called, fights Cleveland Williams in November 1966.

Clay joined the Black Muslims and adopted the name Muhammad Ali. In 1967, after successfully defending his title in a 15-round fight with Ernie Terrell, Ali received his draft papers. He refused to go into the army on religious grounds, was stripped of his title and barred from the ring. Always the fighter, Ali took his case to the U.S. Supreme Court and his title was restored to him in 1970.

Ali lost the title to Joe Frazier in 1971 in one of the best world title fights ever. Three years later, he won his title back again in an eight-round thriller against George Foreman. But in 1978, he lost the title again, on a points decision, to Leon Spinks.

Incredibly, Ali won the title back a few months later. He is the only man ever to have won the title three times.

Ali used to boast, "I am the greatest." Experts think he probably was.

Bob WOODWARD (b. 1943) ★★★

Carl BERNSTEIN (b. 1944) ★★★

The reporters who brought down a President

★

On Sunday, June 17, 1972, President Nixon read in the *Miami Herald* that five men had been arrested in the Democratic National Committee HQ in The Watergate, in Washington. He thought little more about it.

But two reporters, Bob Woodward and Carl Bernstein, who had also reported the story in the *Washington Post*, thought there was more to the story than a simple break-in.

Woodward and Bernstein at the Washington Post *offices.*

It turned out that the arrested men had been caught planting bugging equipment in the Democrat Party's headquarters. Woodward and Bernstein began to investigate the story in depth. They interviewed anyone who they thought could give them information. They followed up every lead.

As word of their investigation spread throughout Washington, a mysterious stranger, known only as "Deep Throat," contacted them to tell them they were on the right track. As the investigation proceeded, "Deep Throat" gave them more and more information. Bernstein and Woodward reported that authority for the Watergate break-in had come from someone in high office at the White House, and that a secret "slush" fund existed to get Nixon re-elected. This meant that bribery was almost certainly occurring.

Nixon was re-elected in the fall of '72. His second term of office was dominated by the Watergate scandal. A Senate committee was called to investigate the affair. The Attorney-General, John Mitchell, was implicated in the scandal. So was Nixon's personal legal advisor, John Dean, who told the committee that all the president's phone-calls were

Richard Millhouse Nixon, the President they exposed.

on tape. Nixon was ordered by the Supreme Court to hand the tapes over. They proved, to the satisfaction of most Americans, that Nixon had been involved in trying to cover up White House involvement in the Watergate Affair. He resigned on August 9, 1974.

Things may well have been different if it had not been for the dedicated way in which Woodward and Bernstein followed up the apparently harmless break-in at Watergate.

Their book, *All the President's Men*, became a best-seller and was made into an excellent movie starring Robert Redford and Dustin Hoffman.

Joe ★★★★★★★★★★

NAMATH (b. 1943) ★★★★★★

Football's "Broadway Joe"

★

Joe Namath was one of football's greatest stars. From 1965-1977 he was the New York Jets' quarterback. His style of play won him countless fans among the men, and his film-star good looks made him popular with women all over America.

When Namath retired from the game he featured in the movie *Avalanche Express* in 1978. In 1979, he made his first stage appearance in *Picnic*. This was followed by *Li'l Abner, The Caine Mutiny Court Martial, Sugar,* and in 1981 he starred in a revival of *Damn Yankees,* playing not a football player, but a baseball player.

Namath has been honored with many awards, including Most Valuable Player of Super Bowl, 1969, the Most Courteous Athlete Award and was named to the Sports Hall of Fame in 1981.

Namath has always tried to put back into sport as much as he got out of it. He has even established a scholarship for women athletes at his old college, the University of Alabama.

Joe Namath – great footballer.

LASSIE (b. 1943)

Hollywood's favorite dog

★

Lassie first hit the screen in 1943 in a movie called *Lassie Come Home.* In the film, Lassie, a handsome collie dog, overcomes all the odds to rejoin the owners she had been parted from.

One film critic was moved to call the dog "Greer Garson in furs." The film was so successful that six sequels were made, the last in 1951.

In 1947, Lassie got her own radio show on ABC. From 1954 through 1972 she was the star of a TV series, and later, a cartoon series based on her adventures.

In 1978, Lassie made her big screen comeback when she appeared in *The Magic of Lassie* with James Stewart. Nothing was too good for the dog: When she was in New York to promote the movie, she stayed in a $380-a-day suite at the Plaza Hotel.

Actually, there was more than one Lassie. All her roles were, in fact, played by male dogs! They were all descended from the original canine star – a dog called Pal.

Lassie, film star extraordinaire.

Bruce

SPRINGSTEEN (b. 1949)

"The Boss"

Bruce Springsteen was born in Freehold, New Jersey. He was always a rebel. He remembers one of the nuns at his school trying to stuff him into a garbage can because, as she explained, "That's where you belong."

When he was nine, Springsteen saw Elvis Presley on television. The next day, he picked up a guitar for the first time. But he put it down straight away – he couldn't play it. Later, however, he saved $18 to buy his own, and by the late 1960s he was playing clubs in New York and New Jersey, either solo or with rock bands.

A combination of bluff, determination and talent got Springsteen a record deal with CBS. His first album, *Greetings from Asbury Park N.J.*, was released in 1973 – the rest is history.

When *Born in the USA* was released in 1984 it sold 1 million copies within 48 hours. Springsteen has been on top for more than 10 years, and will most likely stay there for many years to come.

Bruce Springsteen's most popular hit must surely be "Born to Run."

Mark

SPITZ (b. 1950)

The best Olympic swimmer of all time

★

When Mark Spitz, an 18-year-old Californian, was picked to swim for the United States at the 1968 Olympics, he upset many people by openly boasting that he would win six gold medals. They thought it served him right when he only won two, plus a silver and a bronze.

Spitz kept his opinions to himself when he was chosen for the 1972 Olympic squad and he won every gold he could: 100 and 200 meter freestyle, 100 and 200 meter butterfly, 100 meter relay freestyle, 200 meter relay freestyle and 100 meter relay medley. All in world record times.

Spitz returned to America a hero. A lifesize poster of him wearing his seven gold medals sold 300,000 copies in just eight months.

Within five years, all Spitz's records had been broken, but he will long be remembered as the greatest Olympic swimmer of all time.

After retiring from the sports scene, Spitz returned to his full-time profession – as a dentist!

★

Mark Spitz (center) wins gold at the 1972 Munich Olympics.

★★★★★★★★★★★
MADONNA (b. 1958) ★★★★★

The biggest-selling female singer in the world
★

Louise Veronica Ciccone was 19 when she flew from her home town, Detroit, Michigan, to New York City, determined to make it as a dancer. She had $35 in her pocket.

After studying with Alvin Ailey, working in doughnut stores, spending a brief time as assistant to choreographer Pearl Lange and a short spell in Paris, she joined a band called The Breakfast Club. By the time the band broke up she had decided she could make it on her own as a singer – named Madonna.

Madonna was on the breadline, living on a diet of peanuts and yogurt, until one of her demo discs was heard by an A & R (Artist and Repertoire) man from Sire Records. She was promptly signed.

Sire Records released two 12-inch singles and, encouraged by their success, released an album, simply called *Madonna*. It sold 2 million copies. Madonna's debut concert tour sold out in record time. Her film, *Desperately Seeking Susan*, was a huge success. And, in 1985, Madonna received an accolade reserved for only a few – she appeared on the front cover of *Time* magazine.

Madonna, the queen of pop.

Michael

JACKSON (b. 1958)

The man who made *Thriller*

★

It was Michael Jackson's father, Joe, who suggested his five sons get together to form a singing group.

In 1968, The Jackson Five sang at a political rally on the same bill as Diana Ross and the Supremes. Within weeks of that gig they recorded their first hit single, *I Want You Back*.

The Jackson Five went on to become one of the most successful groups of the 1970s, and then Michael became one of the most successful solo recording artists in history. His third single, *Ben*, reached number one in October 1972. His 1979 album, *Off the Wall*, sold 8 million copies. But that was nothing compared to the success of *Thriller*. It was released on December 1, 1982, and sold an incredible 38.5 million copies.

In 1984, Jackson was badly burned while filming a television ad for Pepsi-Cola. But two years later, the company asked him to endorse their drink and agreed to pay him $50 million to do so.

★

Michael Jackson in concert.

John  ★★★★★★★★★★★

McENROE (b. 1959) ★★★★★

Tennis "super-brat"

★

Experts agree John McEnroe is one of the greatest tennis players ever. Spectators agree he is one of the most exciting to watch. But umpires and linesmen probably agree he is the most difficult player ever to cope with on court.

McEnroe stunned the tennis world in 1977 when, having had to qualify for the Wimbledon tournament in England, he reached the semi-finals. Two years later, he won the U.S. Open. He won Wimbledon in 1981, 1983, and 1984, and the U.S. Open in 1980, 1981, and 1984.

But McEnroe has an explosive temper and has several times been fined for his behavior on court.

Tennis fans hoped McEnroe's marriage to Tatum, Ryan O'Neil's daughter, would calm him down, but he has been involved in several on and off-court disputes since then.

By 1987, McEnroe's appearances suggested his best playing days were behind him. But he will always be remembered as one of the greatest American tennis stars of all time.

★

John McEnroe, tennis megastar.

Capt. James T.

★★★★★★

KIRK (b. circa 2100)

★★★★★★

The man who's boldly gone where no man has gone before

★

Thanks to the miracles of modern technology, 20th-century television viewers and movie-goers have been able to follow the 22nd-century adventures of Capt. James T. Kirk and the crew of the Star Ship *Enterprise*.

Kirk, ably supported by his Chief Engineer Scotty, Second Officer Spock (half human and half Vulcan), and the crew's medical officer, known to one and all as Bones, has taken his ship to the edges of the universe, visiting galaxies where no human has previously set foot, facing danger with great calm.

Kirk first hit our television screens in 1966. Seventy-nine episodes of the series *Star Trek*, which chronicles Kirk's adventures, have been made. They have been shown over and over again in more than 52 countries. One U.S. station has shown an episode every day for more than 10 years.

"Trekkies" were pleased when Kirk and his crew made their first feature movie in 1973. More followed, and we hope that the brave captain will continue to beam back to Earth many more of his adventures.

William Shatner plays Capt. James T. Kirk of the Starship Enterprise.